BEYOND BULLFIGHTS AND ICE HOCKEY

Essays on Identity, Language and
Writing Culture

paulo da costa

ISBN: 0996051139
ISBN-13: 978-0996051132

CONTENTS

To the Reader

(who in these times of no time has dared to take the time
for a long visit to another mind)

Never be a spectator of unfairness or stupidity. Seek out argument and disputation for their own sake; the grave will provide plenty of time for silence.

— Christopher Hitchens, *Letters to a Young Contrarian*

Until we know the assumptions in which we are drenched, we cannot know ourselves.

— Adrienne Rich, *When We Dead Awaken: Writing as Re-Vision*

"Son los árboles que dan frutos los que sufren las pedradas."

— Eduardo Galeano, *Patas Arriba*

FOREWORD

For those who believe the book is obsolete and has been overtaken by other cultural platforms and technologies in our increasingly fast-moving times, I remind myself that the book is a marker of sanity for the human spirit. It will always be a measure of how far we humans have fallen off our cultural and spiritual balance. The book is an intimate match to the rhythm of our consciousness, our state of being present in the world, our hunger to see and be seen, to hear and be heard.

In this fast-paced life, we can reach many places yet experience little, we can move faster and overlook more, we can chase our tales and never have our heart touched. The book is a narrative, a conversation, a painting in words that slows us down, teaching us to pay attention. The book is not dying, what is dying is a way of being attuned to slowness; a slowness that once brought us deeper consciousness and awareness, the value of being present with each other and the world. What is dying is the quality of "being present" that brought us fulfillment and now in its absence, leaves us vacant and spinning, attempting to fill our hearts and spirits with more of everything, while we feel hollower than ever. Fulfillment in the human experience is not about quantity. The quality of the human experience is the secret to immortal awe. The book will remain a signpost and will await our return to a balanced existence. The book is not in a hurry to prove its value in our lives. In the same way, a sitting meditation never feared the automobile that promised to take us farther, faster and show us more. After exploring every corner of the globe, the traveler still returns to the meditation cushion, to sit and gaze deeper, slower, and longer inside the mind and the heart.

paulo de costa

Vancouver Island, Canada 2014

IDENTITY

WINTER KALE AND THE OLD MAN

Portraits of Queen Elizabeth the Second in full regalia lined the walls. The oil paintings spanned the mood of her reign. Sixty prospective citizens stood, left hands raised, their free hands clutching Korans, Bibles, Books of Mormon. I clutched a pine cone in my vest pocket.

"I swear I will be faithful and bear true allegiance to her Majesty Queen Elizabeth the Second, Queen of England, Her Heirs and Successors, according to law and that I will faithfully observe the laws of Canada and fulfil my duties as a Canadian citizen."

Soon-to-be citizens, and eager relatives, repeated in unison, line by line, the required oath while I practised the liberties granted by the Charter of Rights, framed in gold behind me: freedom of conscience, belief, opinion, and expression. So, I moved my lips, without sound, as a fish speaks on dry land. Half a sentence did not compromise my integrity: "Fulfilling my duties as a Canadian citizen." A loose enough uniform that would not confine my movement or constrict my body of beliefs.

I had no desire to swear blind allegiance to compulsory Kings or Queens. I could make up my own mind about who to trust, thank you very much. The thought of becoming a colonial British subject irritated me. I had never been a believer there was a difference, grammatical or otherwise, between subject and object as exemplified by ex-radio announcers, ex-football players and ex-movie stars turned politicians. What if the Royal family, crazed from centuries of inbreeding, declared war on my sister and my country across the ocean? I had already fled a Continent where one demonstrated love of country by the willingness to be trained in the art of shedding blood. Loving a nation meant loving it to death.

"It is with extraordinary pleasure that I welcome you to this final step into the Canadian family." The judge sat poised and dignified, giving solemnity to the occasion. A touch of friendliness punctuated her speech.

I supposed they considered me an adopted child of this extended Canadian family. As with any family, I stepped into the dynamics of favouritism, unspoken shame, obedience, rewards, punishments, the dark secrets rusting behind the painted facade of family life. Its crumbling values were still cherished, its faults glossed over—a flawless and framed family portrait.

A thunderous voice interrupted my musings and commanded, "Everyone smile." The whitewash of a camera flash blinded me. Tentative flags waved. A few of us would join the growing ranks of runaways, black sheep, forgotten daughters, scapegoats. As with any dysfunctional family, Canada suffered from the malaise of intimate urban living, a daily friction without a common language of the heart, a language to peel off the lies and the suffering with the breath of tenderness. A sense of guilt overwhelmed me. What if people could read my mind—would they accuse me of being difficult, of being disloyal? I did not want to sound ungrateful. "Be positive. Everything in the world is precisely as it's supposed to be," a new friend, twirling a glimmering quartz crystal on her necklace, had recently counselled.

Centuries from now, would historians accuse me of being an accomplice to the decimation of North America's indigenous cultures through the slow, agonising process of colonisation? They could never accuse me of bare-handed murder; but perhaps I exterminated them with the automobile roads where I drove, the semi-attached house by the river, the getaway cabin in the woods, the parks I hiked on weekends, the innocent and banal activities of modern life.

I examined the sober dignitaries in the courtroom, the aligned chairs, the polished brass, the ironed skirts and pressed suits. I would have preferred a First Nations welcome. I pictured us huddled in the womb of a sweat lodge, our faces radiant from the incandescent rocks. An elder, not in a black robe, but a cape of cedar bark, recited prayers and offered tobacco. The burning sweetgrass bundle passed, hand to hand, bathing us in smoke. Water, splashed over a shallow pit of glowing rocks, rose to steam, a burst of breath searing against our chests. Our mouths hung ajar, thirsty for truth. The sweat invited the skin, the entire body, to speak. Expatriating the sweat left a lighter spirit behind. Four rounds, four directions, four races, and after the cleansing and eating, cleared bodies soared in dance.

"Faithfully observe the laws of Canada, faithfully observe the laws of Canada," the chorus of new citizens' voices echoed in my skull and reminded me of a recent newspaper headline. The story of a pristine town, nestled among glaciers, awakened by a decree to chlorinate their water for the well-being and safety of its citizens, to comply with elevated health standards. The townspeople revolted, marched in the streets. They would not bleach their water—already pure enough that Australia and Japan paid high prices to have it bottled and exported. The police force arrived to instill order, to distill and dilute the lawbreakers. What were people to do when the law forbade the sane and fair? Had Canada no room for Robin Hoods? I wished I had worn my *Question Authority* button, the one that had prompted a co-worker to ask in fear, "You're going to be a good Canadian citizen and stay out of trouble, aren't you?" "And what about the attack on universal health care and social programs by business tycoons disguised as politicians?" "You shouldn't complain. Be thankful you aren't dying on the streets of Sarajevo or starving to death in Ethiopia. If things look so bad here, you are always welcome to return home," my co-worker voiced in response. Perhaps I did not have a right to complain, to dream of justice and freedom, to believe the world could be improved. Perhaps I should be content, and cherish the fact I did not live as a Roman or African slave. "Perhaps this country offers the freedom we enjoy because of those who stood up for something and took nothing for granted." I invited her to join me in a public protest at McDougal Square. She declined. She had plans to work on her suntan at Sandy Beach.

A maple leaf flag drooped to the left of the courtroom where a Mountie stood.

"All rise, this Court is coming to order," the Mountie had said when the judge first walked in. Through the ceremony he stood to the side, a postcard in a Banff shop window, a national symbol, serious and charming. If it were not for the Mounties I would not be in the Citizenship Court. Mounties opened up Western Canada. Everything that is opened up bleeds, I know. The Mountie's scarlet military uniform, held together along his chest by shiny golden buttons, sent shivers down my spine.

"The things we value are the things we take most for granted. Let us remember that multiculturalism rests at the heart of every Canadian. I am of Scottish ancestry, but I am also Korean, Portuguese, Venezuelan, and every other ethnic background that populates this country," the judge reminded us.

I surveyed the courtroom. Two dozen countries were represented in a wide spectrum of shades, shapes and sizes, as most stood in a sameness of suits and ties, dresses and high heels; nervous, hoping not to stand out, obeying new social rules. The summoning notice to the ceremony had reminded us to dress accordingly. According to what?

I wondered what forced the other new Canadians to sever their roots and flee familiar soil. I wondered what injuries they carried in their silence. I wondered if the woman in dreadlocks, in the front row, had refused to answer phones, afraid, as I had been, of messing up the accurate relay of messages. Canadians spoke in the same hurried manner used for walking from store to store, breathless. Callers' sentences would twist and turn in my mind, lost in the labyrinth of possible meanings. The caller would hang up in frustration.

An older man, darkened by a sun-dyed lineage, stood guarded, arms crossed over his heart, his eyes escaping through the window. Longing for a faraway land, he released a faint smile. Had he also arrived on a 30-below night? I discovered a snow-covered city, foreign to the touch. No resemblance to the alluring Hollywood movies where people stuck their tongues out to nibble on floating snowflakes. No resemblance to Christmas cards where people tobogganed on slopes, spilling their joyous laughter, and moulded spontaneous snow angels in the white fluff. Not the colourful television commercials that presented adults riding in sleighs and singing Christmas Carols while their children rolled snow, building fantasies that would, in time, melt. Coming from the airport, through the deserted downtown streets of ice, my eyes searched for carollers, skating children. Instead, scattered sheets of newspaper twirled in a black and white scene of huddled bodies sleeping over steam-exhaling street vents. A desolate landscape. I pressed my nose against the car window, the glass cold enough to freeze my tears. Words wilted in my dry throat. The wind outside howled for me.

Minus thirty. I had phoned home.

My mother's all-knowing voice insisted that human beings were not created to live in such miserable conditions. "There must be a mistake," she said without hesitation, "A different scale, Fahrenheit, isn't it?"

"Minus thirty is cold for any scale," I told her in our mother tongue. "Your choice," she reminded, adding that back home it had been an average winter day. Plus 14. "I've never seen frozen water outside a freezer. Can you smell the *caldo verde* simmering on my stove?"

"Of course, mother. It's minus thirty!" I recalled the scent of olive oil perfuming stripped kale and pureed potatoes.

The day of my arrival became the coldest, longest day in memory, even though the mercury sank far deeper later that month. Along the route from the airport I had searched for the comfort of red-tiled rooftops, overhanging grapevines. Instead, I saw frosted windows and countless neon donut signs. I wanted to ask what donuts were. In my understanding, something sold by the dozens, intrinsic to the culture. I expected to try donuts soon. Years later, I could not bear the thought of donuts, the overly glossed topping, the hole, the emptiness in the middle.

This emptiness in my chest numbed my spirit. An unrelenting squeeze of tight anxiety—the way a mustard bottle is shaken and squeezed for its last drop, before it's refilled.

In those first few months I had found it impossible to laugh. The sky ranged from near black, to lighter grey. After a while, I shut the blinds and curled in bed teaching myself English. I refused to step outside alone. I read everything I could find on the pioneers, the true North. I wanted to know everything about Canada, to ensure that the day I walked out the front door everything would be perfect. On rare outings, I fretted between style and comfort when selecting my clothes. I didn't want people peering at me sideways, too polite to stare, but treating me as an alien from a distant galaxy.

At the bottom of my green duffel bag, I found the lost envelope of kale seeds my grandfather had tucked in my breast pocket on our last embrace before my departure. I sifted the round black seeds on the palm of my hand before I let them escape through my open fingers into the large pot inside the balcony window. I opened the window blinds again.

The seclusion and reading did nothing but delay the inevitable. In my first solitary foray into downtown I lost my bearings and sought refuge in a phone booth. The coin slot appeared in the wrong place, the beeping sounded peculiar, my coins were eaten without result. I read the instructions in the phone booth until I could recite them from memory, still not understanding them. A knock on the door. "Hurry up, it's not a wind shelter. Make up your mind!" I exited, staring at my snow-covered boots. Trendy at home, "dirt ballish" here, a passerby had informed me.

I wandered dusk-filled, otherwise empty streets. The street numbers twisted my mind, 108th Avenue, 8th Street. I had grown accustomed to street names that led people down paths of cultured time and history; avenues to revolutionaries, poets, painters, sculptors, doctors and saints. Gazing at a street name painted on bluish tile, I felt connected. Those long twisting streets stretching out of sight were a continuum that spanned past to future. I belonged. In Canada, avenues went sideways, streets up and down. Coordinates on a map. Maps were pictures in my head, not numbers. "But it's easier, any stranger can find their way in this city. It's impossible to get lost," an acquaintance explained. A strange place or a place of strangers, I wondered. A figment of geometry, an imaginary plane.

"Citizenship is the highest honour a country bestows on an individual." The speech concluded. Dutiful applause.

One by one, the new Canadians were called by their full names to the court bench and handed a certificate by the judge. Local dignitaries stood in Indian file to shake our hands. Indian file! From my gut rose nauseating memories of John Wayne matinees.

In a strange accent the judge called my name, and I almost missed myself in the echo of twisted sounds. I shuffled to the front dragging the length of my name: Soares, going back to my great-great-grandmother on my mother's side; Alves, from my grandmother on my father's side; da Costa, my father's lineage, a long thread extending, resisting, pulling me back to a homeland of ancient lore. I approached the court bench and the judge stared at my hand-painted T-shirt showing three desperate wolves howling at the full, silent moon. I wanted to ask her if the wolves would qualify for a wallet-size citizenship card, too. The eager new Canadians shuffled their impatient feet behind me. I did not want to upset her. I smiled, and obedient, returned to my seat. I already fit in. From now on all my revolutions would be private, sheltered in the safety of my voiceless thoughts.

Everyone rose to sing the national anthem.
    I sang.
    "Oh Canada! My home not native land . . ."
    My first months in the new land had reminded me of my grandfather's final years. He had complained that technology did not make sense in his life—telephones, the voices of the grandchildren he never saw, black and white photographs, images of a son deployed to war who for years he could not embrace. My grandfather lived his last years within unfamiliar walls, walls void of his past, void of shared memories. He mourned his straw mattress and now lay on a new, stubborn mattress that resisted the weight and shape of his body and kept him awake through the night. His insomnia paced among the trinkets he stopped trusting, had never switched on or could not imagine a use for. He could not be bothered. For lack of things to do he overwatered his kale plants. His lifelong bearings had been turned upside down. Everything changed too fast, always for the worse. He died of a broken heart with his plants by his bedside and a postcard I had sent him that week tucked in his chest pocket.
    For the people standing in the courtroom, homesickness revealed a minor ailment in comparison to the nightmares of violence, love, or both, they had fled. True believers, of deep faith, optimists at heart, these were the new Canadians. Their vision of hope undefeatable. The citizenship ceremony

marked the first official breath of their reincarnation.

New sounds, new words. On my tongue the words of a child, and people did not tire of telling me so: "A pre-schooler's syntax and the vocabulary of a nine-year-old. How charming!" They spoke to me in the condescending tone reserved for children, for the mentally challenged. They believed that what I could express revealed everything I knew.

My legs carried me over the treacherous contours of new land. Every couple of blocks a slippery patch of black ice inflicted more pain on my body, another bruise to my dignity. Legs with a mind of their own. Who was I? Legs of a toddler, words of a pre-schooler, mind of a teenager. A Frankenstein assembled from bits and pieces. Patched here, tied up there, mended everywhere. A post-modern or a post-mortem spirit? I learned the meaning of slush, crusts, flurries, quinsy, icicles, fluff. I learned the meaning of black ice. A reassembled world started to gain new contours. Even if slippery.

"Welcome to Canada. You are now full citizens of this vast land. May your dreams come true. Cake and tea will be served in the foyer." The judge stood and exited with the pomp of a trumpet. Everyone followed suit.

When I escaped from the city, I liked the colours before me, and the sky wide as the ocean I missed. So near to my head I jumped up in the air ready to dive in. I giggled at the sight of coyotes trotting across fenced fields with *No Trespassing* signs; delighted in the sound of hawks pitching their warning cry to quaint groundhogs standing in the ditch.

I began to like the people. They stopped their cars the moment my foot touched the crosswalk. Every second sentence carried a please or a thank-you. My inadvertent step on someone's toes prompted their immediate and profuse apology. Easy smiles, immaculate teeth. Back home people did not smile as often, missing front teeth, brows furrowed from the weight of *saudade,* clenching the memory of children never returned from the battlefield; although a few resilient smiles carried contagious laughter and commotion. In the new country I grew accustomed to silent Charlie Chaplin smiles.

I lounged in bed, leaned against the wall, writing cheerful letters home. I silenced the old man in me and allowed the child, the invincible optimist, the discoverer - to speak. I didn't want my family to worry. They missed me. Had they ever used chopsticks to eat? Ukrainian perogies were my first meal in Canada. Potato-filled dough in the shape of my favourite rissoles. Did they know what a burrito was? Of course not. No, not a donkey. "Is there any true Canadian food?" my mother asked. Maple syrup, I supposed. I told her I slept on a futon—a Japanese bed, hard cotton mattress so low to the floor it squeezed out any lingering ghosts. Every day I experimented with new trinkets. Electric toothbrushes, electric can openers, electric ice-scrapers. With faith in the modern, my new self pushed forth into the New World, leaving behind the old man who stared at tins of food in the cupboard and remembered war rations. The tins full of unidentifiable mush, salty to the lips. Deadly.

The old man in me walked to the balcony window and watered the kale in the pot. After having struggled to break through the surface, the kale already displayed its double, green face in the two tender leaves. It would not grow tall and bushy in the confines of a pot. However, it would grow.

The child in me returned to the cupboard door left ajar and shut the sight of the canned food. Exuding faith, the child stared at the calendar pinned against the cupboard door. Looked ahead to the end of the month, to a new holiday, a new custom to celebrate. Halloween.

"Trick or treat?"

A seven-year-old Queen Victoria stood at my door, hand outstretched. Sweet enchanting smile. An aluminum foil crown and brilliantine hair, glittering with glamour and pose.

"Trick or treat?" she insisted.

I filled her hands with candy. She bowed and disappeared on tiptoes.

From my partner's closet I borrowed a Charleston dress from the twenties. I walked to the bathroom and held it against my body. I checked my profile in the wall mirror. A swing of my hips and the frills swayed in a beautiful arc. I rolled black panty-hose up my legs. Hairs poked through the holes. A long pearl earring dangled from my earlobe. I slid grapefruits into the breast hollows and ran the back of my hand over my six o'clock shadow. It scraped my hand. I shaved.

Bright rouge lipstick glided onto my lips. I smooched and kissed a serviette to dry the excess moisture. Kissed another tree good-bye. Tinted my eyelashes, rubbed a light touch of blush on my cheeks. A snug, red boa warmed my neck. I readjusted the fake diamond tiara. Stretched my arms. The evening gloves concealed my hairy arms. In the mirror I snapped a polaroid to send home. I did not recognise myself. I laughed and walked to the balcony window scrutinising the white prairie, the limitless horizon. I laughed again, fluffed my wig's golden locks and howled with the hungry wolves camouflaged and invisible on the winter prairie.

The old man in me stared at my body-tight dress and shook his head. Then, he stared into the snow-covered prairie and knew that even his favourite resilient kale would never survive the white-out of Canadian winter.

Calgary / 1993

BEYOND BULLFIGHTS AND ICE HOCKEY
-AN ARCHITECTURE OF MULTICULTURAL IDENTITY-

Homens que são como lugares mal situados
Homens que são como casas saqueadas
[…]
Homens encarcerados abrindo-se com facas
Homens que são como danos irreparáveis
Homens que são sobreviventes vivos
Homens que são como sítios desviados
Do lugar

(excerpto de poema)
Daniel Faria

People who are like poorly situated places
People who are like ransacked houses
[…]
Incarcerated people opening themselves
with knives
People who are like irreparable damage
People who are living survivors
People who are like places hijacked
From place

(excerpt from untitled poem)
 Daniel Faria
translated by paulo da costa

My first memories, first smells and sounds are of Angola, coloured by its African geography of heat and flavoured by its culture, spirituality and music. My experience of the continent was brief, since a handful of years later my parents returned to their homeland in Portugal, where I was raised in the northern grape-growing hills of Beira Litoral. Backpack on my shoulders, I began travelling on my own at the age of fourteen, first within Portugal and soon into the rest of Europe and the gates of Asia. Later, with my first steps into adulthood, I travelled and worked around the world for four years, having along the way also lived and worked in Canada, England and Australia. After seeing chunks of the planet and crisscrossing several longitudes and latitudes, I elected Canada as my desired place to drop new roots. I have chosen to live in this country, Canada, because I cherish a society where cultural diversity is encouraged.

I presume that I have struggled with challenges similar to those faced by immigrants anywhere. Issues of identity; of belonging and alienation; of integration, assimilation, and yes, also resistance to my country of *acolhimento*—shelter. I have boomeranged between Canada and Portugal while feeling neither Portuguese nor Canadian, and longing for that which I perceived missing on either side. In my state of separation, I have experienced torment and confusion, feeling separate from either culture. Exacerbating the experience, people have at times related to me as though I might be an alien, my voice revealing the accent of a newcomer.

With time, I realized I undermined myself by accepting other people's views of me as my own. I realised I was the one uncertain of who I was, the one who accepted their vision of myself. I began to find peace and balance when I refused to fit myself to the real or perceived demands from the state, the community and the nations on either side of the Atlantic, and refused accepting their expectations and judgments as my own. I know now I am the one who can change what I feel about who I am. This metamorphosis began by accepting the differences and contradictions within me. I now feel 100% Canadian and 100% Portuguese, and no one else can alter that feeling. I will present you with a poem that might illustrate my arrival at this new understanding of myself.

*

vive

    entre portugal e canadá

   touradas e hóquei no gelo
    bacalhau e salmão

     o que se traduz por um viver
  itinerante e impertinente

vive

    naquela nuvem de alta ou baixa
pressão
naquele espaço impermanente
   sem raízes e ervas daninhas

    formas, identidades e
pensamentos
reinventam-se com os ventos

    materializam-se e evaporam-se
nas rugas do atlântico

vive

    nessa nuvem sem bandeiras
onde a trovoadas deixa de ser
   o embate de hinos

*

he lives

    between portugal and canada

   bullfights and ice hockey
    cod and salmon

    which translates as itinerant
and impertinent living

he lives

    in that high and low pressure
cloud
in that impermanent space
   without roots and weeds

    forms, identities and
thoughts
reinvented with the winds

    materialise and evaporate
in the furrows of the atlantic

he lives

    in that cloud without a flag
where thunder is no longer
   the clash of anthems

Diversity, as important in the construct of an individual identity as in the larger society, implies a vision of multiculturalism beyond clustered and isolated cultural islands dotting a country. I propose a multiculturalism rooted in the individual rather than the group, a personal cultural mosaic allowing you and me to interweave and belong to a complex hive of cultural heritages, languages and relationships.

I write in either English or Portuguese, as my mind travels the two linguistic landscapes. I know some of you do not speak or understand Portuguese; therefore at times I will translate the Portuguese. At other times I will not. I believe it is important to experience the sounds and sights of unfamiliar tongues, to embrace the experience of not knowing. I trust that meanings will surface as you observe the unfamiliar words of Portuguese. We can practice not understanding another and still be present for the experience.

In my life, I have engaged in a conscious effort to question the inherited values of cultural heritage and not merely swallow them through habituation. I want my values, including my cultural values, to reflect my conscious choices. This work of filtering and evaluating the cultural air one breathes and of making conscious choices is lifelong and requires stamina and perseverance. At the same time the recompense is exquisite. Culture is not born of immaculate conception or genetically acquired; it reflects the time and effort invested in cultivating its practice. Identity unfolds in action. As I choose to see myself as 100% Canadian and 100% Portuguese, I need only to share some of its traits to feel my full membership. I am an atypical Portuguese and an atypical Canadian. I am a Portuguese who has not eaten meat for twenty years, who eats olives for breakfast, dresses in all the colours of the rainbow. I am an odd Canadian too, one who does not apologize when, on a crowded bus, the person next to me has just stepped on my foot. I do not play the 6/49 lottery or watch ice hockey. It is my participation at a political, social and community level that provides me with cultural membership in the Canadian and Portuguese societies. I am an engaged citizen in both cultures. I no longer need to be glued tight on all sides of my being to feel connected and to discover a sense of belonging to either culture.

It is ironic that I did not identify with the culture that surrounded me while growing up in Portugal. I did not find expression and connection to the predominant culture's values. I grew up in a time where bullfights were broadcast weekly on Portuguese TV during bullfighting season. I did not, however, partake of the joy expressed by family and friends while watching a corralled animal subjected to torture and suffering for human pleasure and entertainment. I did not find an echo of myself in such a cultural practice, nor in many other practices and values that promote narrow lines of identification, supposedly common to all citizens and unquestionably shared. It was only after I had left Portugal, travelled and lived in other parts of the globe that I found connection to my cultural identity as Portuguese—an identity that I felt did not have to prescribe to clichés of identity, or compromise my fundamental sense of difference. In this same vein, I do not see my Canadianness echoed in the general traits of the nation. I enjoy skating on the frozen lakes of the Rockies, gliding under the northern sky, yet I am not a hockey fan. I recognize that such existence reflects a personal comfort in residing on the margins. I value margins, for on the margins one finds room to grow.

With many Portuguese I share an appreciation for particular foods, music and landscapes. That is the case with *broa* (crusty corn bread), the sharp twang of the Portuguese guitar, the resonance of *fado*. This is not to say that all these experiences do not move people from other cultures with equal passion. Many people, regardless of their particular cultural heritage, will appreciate music from Madredeus, Amália and Mariza, or the taste and texture of *broa*. Yet the Portuguese are at present the ones sustaining the creation of these specific cultural expressions and culinary experiences. One day people from other cultures will also sing *fado*, in traditional as well as innovative ways, and then the Portuguese will have to expand their sense of cultural ownership and learn to share our enjoyment of this musical style while welcoming this broader participation in the family of *fado*.

With many Canadians I share the aesthetic love of the wild, even the vanishing sprinkles of forest or prairie in the periphery of our metropolises. I share a sense of hope in the future, the vision of a society where dreams have a fair chance to take root. I share the vision of a caring civil society. This requires my participation in shaping its values and in the building of its dreams. My voice, your voice is important in shaping this future.

What if I refuse to choose between the promoted

divisiveness of us versus them or Portuguese versus Canadian? Instead of torturing myself with choosing allegiance to one and rejection of the other, what if I embraced both? One hundred percent Canadian and one hundred per cent Portuguese, I then enter a third dimension that encompasses both identities. I refuse the contraction required in forcing me to deny and separate from an essence of myself. What if I start to perceive my relationships, my beliefs, and my conduct as embodying this larger self, a posture that will also hold and honour the differences and perhaps contradictions within me? In this manner perhaps I would truly inhabit a poetic life, for poetry is the art of holding the tension of opposites, and this resulting energy nourishes the poet. The poet's language finds a creative illuminating path through the paradox and the ambiguity of being while bringing forth newness: the artist's creation.

As I accept and am true to myself—and by extension, as I accept the billions of other multicultural people on this globe—I must then stand for a vision where we not only learn to coexist in diversity, but also thrive and find our inspiration in the places of synthesis.

Let us not think small, shrink and vanish in the amorphous currents of sameness. We hold tremendous power. Our societies need our participation to be reinvigorated. Let us look at the accomplishments. Multiculturalism, this increased movement and meeting of cultures, ideas, values, has contributed to advances spanning all fields of science and humanities. North America was the most exciting place on earth because of the energy brought by all races and cultures brewing endless vats of newness. In the Canadian literary arts in particular, the establishment seems, in the last couple of decades, at last to be acknowledging the contribution of fusion Canadian writers— those writers who hold in their consciousness more than one culture, and at times, even more than one language. Some of these exciting Canadian voices include Ondaatje, Brand, Mistry and Clarke, to name only a few of our writers who are contributing to the renewal of the English language and literatures around the world. The fusion writers are changing the language, imbuing it with a renewed vitality, a broader palette of colours stemming from our diverse cultural roots. In turn, this process will make the use of English even more prevalent, in particular if it accepts and integrates such new vitality; in turn we will also carry the music and the imprint of English into other tongues in our repertoire.

Imagine the vitality of a new English speaker or narrator when employing language in the following manner.

From

Globotomy
(novel-in-progress)

Elvito Sucumba Ypiranga da Silva Sushioka-Helmut, that's what I was branded the day I was ejected from the slit slot machine of life. Microscopically dissecting at my heritage, you find a shade of everywhere in my name, and furthermore than less, there are extraplus ethnic rainbows on my skin than many another. I'm everyone from allwheres, the future of this contagious continent. And as my marketing professor expelled to our graduating class in his celebrated farewell lecture: own the unique brand that's yourself. And register it, damn it. I suspect that's why this job with the local São Tuatuara newslater media paper has become my trademark.

I'm the prototype journalist who fancies hitting the streets with my soles, listening to the action and reaction of the people on the day, reporting on the eventfuls that shape the facts and contracting the accuracy of the english to inform the world. Living by the sea, my day is never bland. Stepping outside the door to a morning seasoned with brine spray, I walk along Avenida dos Hamburgers with the ocean breeze racing plastic bags along the road. The ocean is ronroning and the reef is peering its head in the distance. The road shuttles back and forth the sound of people chatting on the inexistent sidewalks, going or coming to markets with baskets of fruit and no fish, while juicing the day with pebbles of language, exchanging happiness, disappointments and hopes.

I hope you agree with me that there is energy and inventiveness in the syntax of this text, and in a character who speaks with a polyglot rhythm and vocabulary, informed by a plethora of syntaxes and invented words, while his speech does not obstruct comprehension and therefore communication.

The internal and external contradictions, and the tension that a multicultural individual experiences in spanning more than one language and culture, are not a handicap, rather a gift to ourselves and to society. Let us cultivate and cherish our complexity. This tension is only a burden if unreleased. This tension is the underutilized and blocked energy waiting for a creative use in daily life. For those of us who cultivate a diversity of languages and cultural values it is essential to understand ourselves as holders of an important key to the future direction of our societies. We hold the key to a door of change—change that in time will shift our political process and our governing institutions toward more inclusiveness and cultural sensitivity, and toward deeper degrees of humanness in our institutions.

There is, of course, in our societies negative bias against holding opposite concepts within oneself, to carrying contradictory views or feelings. Such bias is reflected in our language, in expressions such as, "He is of two minds. She is split. I feel divided." For myself I do not see a division in having two minds. I perceive it as an expansion of being.

I gaze at a bridge, and I am reminded of the architecture of a multicultural being. I see the tension required in maintaining this airborne structure stretched between two shores. The bridge is a conduit. We are the translators, the diplomats, the wanderers as well as the inexpensive labourers. We are the links facilitating exchange between cultures; we are merchants of newness, cross-pollinators. We set a society's change and evolution in motion by introducing change. To live on the margin allows us to link and connect the two estranged sides. Do I ask if the bridge belongs to either shore? Do I imagine the bridge divided? Absolutely not. I see the bridge inhabiting a space that rises above the flat geography of boundaries. A bridge crosses chasms at first thought unthinkable. The bridge turns borders obsolete.

I am also aware of the possible risks experienced in the daily life of a fusion-being, the discrimination and exclusion encountered in the minute details of daily life. Modern societies employ force and violence to resist change. We can choose to cultivate the skills and strategies to embrace this multicultural change in ourselves and in our world, or we can chose to resist change and join the ranks of those who live in fear, in smallness and in perpetual defence of the immutable status quo, the fixed coordinates of identity. In time, all status quo collapses under the unstoppable current of change.

It is important for those who understand the beauty contained in diversity to challenge repressive policies of any flavour, to speak and stand up against policies that attempt to homogenise and dishonour our right to difference. We must stand up for practices that accept a more expansive sense of being, practices that include what we have in common rather than reinforcing our differences and what separates us. We must also ease the fear of the unknown in ourselves and in those around us, and face the irrational fear entrenched in the awareness of our difference. Let us then with lavish joy share our differences with the world, not hide or repress them, and demonstrate that there is nothing to be feared and much to be gained. The world of our minds contains sufficient psychic space to accommodate all beings. Let us speak our myriad tongues publically and with pride; let us undertake, and encourage others, to learn more languages. My colourful clothes do not make me dangerous; the spices flavouring my food are not poisonous; my personal values and spiritual beliefs, if they respect plurality of being, can coexist with yours.

And while we promote the differences, let us also remind ourselves of what we have in common. I think it important to focus on what we share across diverse communities rather than focus on our differences in a manner that will separate us.

It is imperative to move beyond the polarisation of an unaccepted duality. When we train ourselves to look at what we have in common, what we share, what brings us together, we might find wonderful surprises. Discovering how intrinsically connected we are to each other, perhaps we will be relaxed enough to accept and encourage each other's differences.

Wittgenstein told us that we couldn't be freed without first being extricated from the extraordinary variety of perceptual associations which hold us prisoner. At this historical juncture it is important to focus on our interconnectedness rather than our differences, without denying or repressing these differences. We can find these points of connection in the most unexpected places. I would like you to read one example from my manuscript of poetry entitled *bifocal* —a collection-in-progress employing only words common to both Portuguese and English, words that can be read in both languages. Though some of those words have identical meanings, many do not. Such is the case with mate and *mate*, or chore and *chore;* words that mean, respectively, kill and cry in Portuguese. Therefore each poem, although in either language appearing identical on the page, will read differently and cast distinct shadows of meaning.

bifocal - viii

angola   romance nostalgia
*   as zebras*
*   no mural*

mosque banana mosquito
aurora   no cinema
*   trio utopia*

ate a zebra
*   no altar*
refute a moral

no crime
*   come*
iguanas   mares
prove trauma - chore
*   refute a moral*

23

Without knowing it, you too were reading Portuguese words on the page even if you missed the particular Portuguese meaning. I dream of one day seeing a world where individuals will speak many tongues, will nurture and explore the heritage of different cultures and still feel connected to that which we share beyond the specificity of any culture: our humanity. I dream of one day living on a planet where most people realize purity is not possible, nor desirable. The quest for purity in history has resulted in bloodbaths, ethnic cleansing, massacres, and the creation of moral monsters such as Hitler or Idi Amin. Change is our ally, the midwife to our unexpressed torments, as long as we embrace it. It allows sustainable and conscious evolution and progress: the expansion of our essence, the expansiveness of our awareness.

I am not oblivious to the cynical voices that murmur in the silence of my mind, and perhaps your mind too, voices insisting that the one who dreams of a world where we lend more weight to our shared experiences than to our differences is a fool. A world where we still cherish and promote those differences is a possible world, and a possible identity. These cynical voices enlist the weight of human history to argue and demonstrate that the human pull towards identity by exclusion will prevail. Those voices think me a foolish dreamer.

I would like to remind myself that I am a poet and a storyteller. My passion is to imagine and create other possible worlds. To dream up possibilities. Not only to point out possible forks in the road, but to carve out those very forks. It is my obligation to recognize what is and then proceed to create what is yet to be. I am in the business of hope.

The weight of history upon our bodies is certainly not stronger than the weight of gravity, and yet for millennia humans have dreamed of one day flying, of taking to the skies in the manner of birds. We dreamed and dreamed in vain, until one day at last we experienced the ecstasy of being airborne. Today, from the hang-glider to the hot-air balloon, from the Boeing to the Space Shuttle, many of us have experienced the exhilarating and the trembling fear of such heights. Any change presupposes a dream, a vision of what might be. A dream requires nourishment, a continuous cultivation of intention. We can indeed change the world by changing how we perceive ourselves, how we act and interact with the world. We must hold such intention dearly, despite the adversities that will challenge our visions. We must persevere until the day we will be released from a particular constraint of history and from a particular perception of ourselves. We can change ourselves and by extension this world, as our changed selves engage in the world; one thought, one word and one action at a time.

I would like to conclude with no conclusion. Instead I offer you a few lines from *"Tabacaria,"* a poem by Fernando Pessoa. Pessoa himself was not content to inhabit one body and one mind, not content to speak one language only, not content to live one life. He created a complex world of heteronyms to expand his human experience. Pessoa challenged the limits of creation by daring to live many lives in one body at one time, allowing him to experience multiple minds, a multifaceted reality, a richly imaginative life. We also may choose to embrace several identities at once, and to carry multiple voices and cultures within us.

I am nothing
I shall never be anything
I cannot wish to be anything.
Aside from that, I hold within me all the dreams of
the world.

Não sou nada.
Nunca serei nada.
Não posso querer ser nada.
À parte isso, tenho em mim todos os sonhos do
mundo.

Cortes Island / 2003

MASS STORYTELLING

Sunday morning in my neighbourhood.

Cars pull into parking lots and doors slam shut. This domino of bangs echoes a timeless, proverbial Big Bang of life-changing events. The amiable people exchange smiles and jovial greetings as they stroll with purpose to their varied gatherings of devotion. In high-ceilinged buildings they will soon congregate and listen to stories of creation, parables of morality, illustrations on righteous conduct. They will sing hymns of worship and pray recurrent supplications for health, wealth and peace.

On the radio, after having rescued the greedy, bankrupt bankers and the automobile barons, another politician extols the value of the goods economy and the economy of good value, while emphasizing the necessity to channel public funds in support of the real economy. I understand the allure of buildings, highways, bridges, automobiles in day-to-day existence. The benefit of such hard-set, long-lasting molecules in constant sight requires no budgetary convincing from politicians. Considering that, in modern nations, CEOs are the ghost writers of the political discourse, the government minister preaches his economic homily on behalf of resource economy executives while justifying another round of cuts to the arts sector, ending "wasteful subsidies for intellectual and artistic privilege." Artists' contributions are subjective, often immaterial, rarely understood. Under his realistic government policies no more fat will pad the cushy life of artistic creation. Were I not in Canada, I might have thought I had travelled back in time to Mao's China or the Khmer Rouge's Cambodia where denigrating and persecuting artists became a fashionable form of target practice. Wait, I was in Canada, with a view of a red maple flag snapping loudly outside the elementary school located across my front door.

Ideology is a charging beast with chopped ears and easy words of advice. A raging bull of self-righteousness on a mission does not listen, sees no red in flags or in flapping *capotes* hiding the deadly *muletas* of *matadores*. For a moment, I consider contacting the radio studio to remind this minister that unlike in politics, the fat of material success remains a rare jackpot in art, and more often than not, wealth arises to those who profit from the posthumous commerce of an artist's fame. Shock more than meditation has trained me to pause and watch the thirty-second train of useless thoughts running over political airtime cliffs; cynicism has taught me that shouting words make little difference to those in power, except on occasion, to break the spell of those hypnotized by the charming promises of the powerful. Instead, I laugh, preserve my precious creative time and decide to speak up on the page, that forum located outside the firing squad of the thirty-second sound *byte* of incomplete thought. The minister will press his words on the wounded art sector: "A relic from fatter times, art must prove its worth in the market place, stand up for itself and sell." In my own mental radio show I tell the minister, "Your flavour of political philosophy has not stopped ministers from handing out indirect subsidies to *certain* private enterprises, from dispensing concessions, research grants or start-up subsidies to a *selected* few or to grant bottled water companies licences to sell us what was already ours." An exception to his ideology of "each standing for itself" applies to most industries in this country. Subsidized stumpage fees for forestry, gas and exploration grants and credits, financial bailouts to big industry. In a minister's mind the money offered to industry represents an investment while money offered to writers represents a handout, a subsistence grant akin to a social program for artists. Hey, who said logic is necessary in the political circus? In the politics of demagogy the art of convincing takes precedence; or generating sufficient background noise to distract, to cover up badly told stories and faulty logic, allows politicians and ministers to get away with indirect murder and a fatter bank account. No Sherlock Holmes mystery in this plot.

Government ministers used to be assigned a portfolio close to their heart. Often artists themselves, with insight into the value of the cultural sector, defended the existence and promotion of culture, suggested policy that safeguarded culture from other clashing interests vying for a share of the cabinet cake. A minister used to be an advocate of his or her cultural portfolio; they used to be a visionary shepherd of the arts. Are ministers now selected for their antagonism to the arts sector? Having their interests and affiliations positioned outside culture, they have become allied to competing interests. Ministers arrive as wolves arrive in a flock—in sheep's skins, soft steps and honeyed words. They arrive to slaughter and pillage.

A minstrel is not a minister, although a minstrel can sometimes be as entertaining, and on the one-dimensional glass screen, the minstrel and the minister become indistinguishable to those who cannot spell. The lean axe has been scraping an artist's bone or chopping their neck from the beginning of time. I have never smelled, nor do I long to smell, the fat of feasts or desserts politicians and industrialists feast on weekly under our tax payer's tab or the deductible loophole of a business meeting; which is to say you and I are subsidizing it either way.

In older times, too, minstrels and storytellers performed for their dinner, but not before everyone else had eaten and been entertained during their meal. Artists are not served first. This remains true in any restaurant that serves food and offers complimentary live music, including political banquets with dignitaries. No, the dignitaries are not the artists. From the beginning of luxurious times, the artists were not considered part of the aristocratic classes of generals and priests, offered chests of gold, country estates or secluded islands as a reward for their services. A certain storyteller of fame was forced to generate a thousand and one nights of stories in order to preserve her neck. I pretend to tell stories to voice the truth; this minister pretends to speak the truth while telling me stories.

The minister holds not the sole responsibility as our candy man, pusher of words and seller of illusions. Remember, it takes two to tango and be taken for a spin. The minister voices everything many want to hear. I would be to blame if I bought it. I am in the line of work of telling the minister and everyone else what they do not want to hear, in contrast to these opportunistic storytellers in the political theatre who spin stories to preserve power, accumulate privilege and reap handsome rewards. Ask a cabinet speech writer who works for the plump actors of parliament and writes what they are ordered to write. I fail to remember a story or parable where, in the span of hundred and one days, a minister or a chief executive must deliver an affordable solar-powered vehicle for the masses in order to preserve their head.

I turn up the radio to better hear my government's cyclical homily of public relations while gazing outside my window. The last trickle of Sunday faithful converge on their respective places of devotion, and my awe grows, as I witness the pull this storyteller named Jesus commands on the minds of the faithful. This is not a run-of-the-mill storyteller. Every

Sunday, he accomplishes an on-going miracle of no small proportions. He inspires people to pause their fast lives, to ponder their life's itinerary, take time aside from their day to sit and listen. Imagine that. Just to listen. Followers will listen with the thirsty eyes of school children with empty minds and hearts, striving to be good (read: to be accepted), to do everything right, wishing to please others (read: to be loved). The devotees converge to their places of devotion, wishing to belong and connect to something other than themselves. Hallelujah, I say. There is hope.

I wonder what is with Sundays and homilies. Are we less busy and more easily persuaded when relaxed? Sundays reinvent my neighbourhood. New faces. Smarter dresses. Subdued ties and sober blues dominate my street landscape. My neighbourhood changes demeanour, and the cars lose their capes of dust. No longer rooted in the physical streets within my visual range, this newly-assembled neighbourhood of belief incarnates a mobile, amorphous entity that appears and disappears with the flicker of the calendar page. I like it. Open markets define the character of any community and bring diverse colours to the social fabric. I would enjoy additional hawkers in our market of belief, competing on equal footing to sell talismans, hawk ideas and promise varied after-futures of hope.

This bestseller storyteller, Jesus, who, in the part of Europe where I grew up, established a monopoly over the creation stories, still enjoys godly status. "I am the way, the truth, and the life ..." he is alleged to have said, and his army of devoted disciples taught me not to listen to any other competing story that suggested alternative imaginings to a narrative of creation. Were I to succumb to the temptation of listening, and also began to believe in other stories, a terrifying plague would afflict me: heresy. The name of this spiritual disease rhymes with cerebral palsy and other debilitating ailments of the body. It does not rhyme with inquisition, banishment and persecution, although these symptoms do follow the disease.

In the same domain of danger as medieval or eternal fire, heresy will not be found in the vicinity of well-behaved boys and girls. Many a time, in my own Sunday school education, I was taught to defend these Jesus stories. As though they incarnated a piece of my body under attack, I was expected to march to war if need be, to save and enlighten infidels and barbarians with my superior truth; this exercise simultaneously determined whose story withstood the test of truth. By means of this civilized crusade and convincing intellectual argument, the winner earns the right to impose their story and establish the truth of the matter. The defeated at once are proven wrong. If a minister says, "God has a beard," and I say, "No, he has a moustache," the minister and I arm-wrestle for the truth until it is proven God indeed wears a beard, because my word stands at Arial twelve while a minister's stands at twelve thousand and one, with ballistic missile range. The defeated in battle are wiser to feign belief and to hasten in practising the rituals of the new story of creation, lest they wake up one morning with no head on their shoulders to enable them to believe in anything at all.

In truth, we Christians only wanted the heretic's land, gold, spices, free forced labour, and slick petroleum. We needed to impose a belief system that legitimized the exploitation of others and each other without revealing the unsightly chains of oppression, the unpleasant exporting of violence; always a distasteful matter to argument and justify just for the sake of greed.

I have been reminded of my location in the hierarchy of storytelling during a Toronto radio show, when a call-in listener reminded me, and every listener, that it was very dandy indeed that my stories received attention and prizes, but all he and everyone else needed to read were the only stories that mattered. No, he had not read my stories. He didn't need to. The only stories that mattered could be found in the Bible. If only people read and re-read them, we would have a perfect world.

Are Jesus stories that remarkable—or has his present

marketing publisher, the Vatican, led by their head-editor *papa* and a legion of post-mortem interpreters of encapsulated meanings simply excelled at promoting his words? Let us not forget the crucial role his first sales team of apostles achieved in the early days. They convinced people that attendance to their Sunday readings remained an essential ingredient in community and personal well-being. Perhaps I should give more credit to the marketeers and the traders; after all, an editor understands what a consumer desires and highlights the message in accordance. At times even shapes it.

Perhaps the pertinence of Jesus' entire two-book collection touches essential aspects of what it means to be human—both old and new editions, also known as testaments. Testament is a heavyweight word to suggest unquestionable reliability as if the statements had been tested—so remarkable that people forget the stories they are and instead read it as an accurate instruction manual, a treatise on humanity, a reflection only the manufacturer of us, the one with insight into the inner working of his inventions, could possibly have mapped. These stories have grown larger than stories and larger than life; through repetition and *massification* they have in time graduated to gospel. I, or you, risk being burnt at the stake of faith for suggesting another possible manner in which stories—including these biblical stories—are true. They are true as literature is true. In their metaphorical amplification, stories become an instrument, both telescopic and microscopic, aimed at the spirit, reflecting and probing the realm of our conscious and unconscious. Imagination is a potent tool to reshape any reality, while it proposes alternative visions for the framework of existence in the world we inhabit.

In all likelihood, the first successful enterprise at branding a storyteller and exporting their message around the world, the Vatican, has created a powerful and planet-wide socio-economic machine of profit. Modern publishers take note. There is a sea of money to be made in stories. Hollywood has also already proven it, and this sea of money is definitely not to be parted with.

I do not wish to belittle the writer or writers of those biblical stories, or their undeniable talent. Many competent writers deliver an enduring story; however, the ability to combine magic tricks involving fish, the vanishing act of a dead body, philosophical depth, poetic morals, and dazzling performance-art drama on a cross, all before a demanding crowd of followers, suggests another dimension—a multidisciplinary genius as relevant as Michelangelo and Da Vinci. Time and distance magnify events, distort memories; as a result, any recounting, any life, any enduring story can be transported to the heights of mythology when expertly maintained alive in the public discourse. The embellished feats, polished colours and supernatural qualities elevate the story to a domain beyond the human scale.

On her way to church, in her velvet dress and purple hat, my neighbour waves. I ponder the reason my stories do not appeal to the masses, and the Sunday ones in particular. No one would attend mass to hear me with the visible devotion shown by those who will regularly attend a rock concert or a spiritual Sunday service delivered by their idols. Meanwhile, to assuage my inadequacies and recurrent doubts as a competent storyteller, I recognize that the marketing machine behind any creation, with its absent or mighty megaphone, has distinct levels of persuasion to beckon readers. The muscle behind the megaphone will press the importance of which stories are a necessary addition to a reader's bedside, and it has often become more relevant to a book's success than the integrity, strength and appeal of its content. The marketeers' spin also imbues the object, say a book, a car, a diamond, with extended magical meaning; it suggests wisdom, power, social status, happiness, and also suggests the transference of these qualities to my life; and since I embody what I believe, the magic will function for a time. When confident, I am larger than myself. The contemporary magicians of darkness labour in the marketing dungeons of corporations, religions and political organizations; they hypnotize and manipulate, they trick and lie to enlist my loyalty to a brand, boss, God, army, identity, idol, work ethic, in order to ease the money from my pocket or gain my political, religious or military allegiance and affiliation—if possible for life or ideally with my life. In church, worshippers believe they receive more than a book: They hold the very word of God.

In my mind, they have turned the paper-thin sliced trees in their hand into a salvation-buoy to float them through the wildest storms of the soul and the free-fall of an empty stomach, and if all proceeds according to Scripture, the best is always yet to come. Just clench your teeth and bear the daily burdens and exploitations.

For the worshippers in that house of transformations, everything carries supernatural powers akin to my childhood castles imparted with extraordinary attributes where dragons would fly, secret passages would open, nature would bend backwards, particularly oceans, potions would transform and expand my one thousand and one limitations. My reality expands as my mind expands. Anything becomes attainable with the right amulets and rituals dispensed for the right price. In the adult castles and sacred forts, drinks of extraordinary powers ferment; songs with magic words open the door to new kingdoms; water rituals purify, offer strength, name and heal me. They will heal, do not misunderstand me. A powerful word or image is transformative, and contains the strength to change my mind and, as a result, to change the chemical and molecular interactions in my body from within and without. My mind creates life and death, and what I believe finds a way to assemble itself into reality. Imagination conveyed through the word is the alchemical element that has been sought from time immemorial, albeit in the wrong place. It is not under the ground or above the cloud. It is not in a powdered flower. It is not in a monkey's testicle, a mushroom's gill, or an elephant's tusk. Alchemy has been under my tongue all along.

It is my tongue. It is the word that paints the imagined vision. Call this magic what you wish. Artists, healers, shamans, even politicians, familiar with this power of creating stories through sounds, words, images, a body in movement, or a combination of all, attempt to reach the senses of those near and far. For the most part they are not heard or they miss the market altogether by believing the free market does not require the expensive keys of marketing to open its door. There is nothing free in this free market.

The last of the faithful have trickled into their place of worship, and outside, the choir of crows and ravens cackling their alms, decisively swoop after the abandoned paper cups, candy and muffin wrappers, chasing the merry dispensations of the modern throw-away-life now twirling in the wind.

I sit at my window longing for these Sunday morning literary readings disguised as religion, and I smile at the people unaware of their resolve to attend the longest-running weekly art performance in the Western world: the communion of old stories retold in modern sacred settings. Enduring, decade-long Broadway hits, pale in comparison. In the centuries before Christ, Greeks congregated in their outdoor theatres, the Aztecs around their temples, the Celts, Haida, Inca, Maori, Tuareg around their bonfires and sacred places, listening to tales of creation. Stitched together, these stories held a sense of this universe through their weave of words—a universe, then and now, still exceedingly enormous for the tiny wings located on each side of our skull that in disconsolation, we resorted to call ears.

The minister on the radio, the minister at the pulpit, and I, we all overlap in our roles. We are in the business of interpreting that which has passed, and that which we witness, all the while proposing a vision for the future. I smile because although I, God, Jesus, and the apostles seem to ply the same line of work ... well, we do not. I am not in the cozy embrace of a centuries-old enterprise delivering the weekly word, wine and bread while fanning the ember of human fears, amassing wealth from our thirst for meaning, mapping the coordinates of the art of living together. I neither have nor wish for a gunpowder-carrying sales team pressing my ideas down the throats of others.

The politician on the radio reminds the listeners that people no longer attend elitist art events such as operas, literary readings, plays, symphonies, while in the silences between the words, he considers artists parasites, and despises their role. In fact, the competition among storytelling venues has increased, as a portable TV and iPod no longer require listeners to congregate and receive stories as a unified community. On both the broadcasting and receiving end, technology provides self-serve storytelling options 24/7. The opera is not alone facing falling attendance. Even the Sunday service storytelling franchise has suffered. The human craving for stories, however, has not diminished and will not. Even the escapist mass sport events, distractions without meaning, end up generating stories, myriad dramas highlighting the prelude and aftermath of games, hooking people to the lives of the protagonists. The game itself is a highly charged drama with a story always delivering a loser and a winner. The human desire to receive a collective experience will return because you and I crave the synergistic power of communion, a collective focus more energizing than a laser beam. The clamour of crowds vibrates our spines, delivers a supernatural charge to the individual cells in my flesh. I crave such strength of communion. I crave it as I crave daily bread. For the time being, sports have replaced churches and musical concerts as the largest source of collective cellular recharging. Places of prayer without intent, stadiums are places of recreation, where the magic of instinct and play reigns. These are not places of invention for the benefit of all. We have been distracted from our creative, imaginative path. We have stopped chewing the peach or kissing the flowers and have been drinking the sugar water from the hummingbird feeder, still believing life is sweet. Nourished we are not. We are rotting from excessive, manufactured sweetness.

As invisible angels, many artists deliver words to the collective unconscious, and people are nourished without knowing they are nourished. Hence my close relationship with the trees I sacrifice daily in my craft. I deliver another type of invisible oxygen that allows for the existence of human spiritual life. Some storymakers probe the depths of beauty, fear, imagination; reflect on human failings and human strengths; warn and encourage. We are not thanked. We do not sell. We are not popular. We are walked over or passed over, sentenced, muffled, destroyed. These storymakers do not sell out, however. We share the fate of the trees and of the forests who stand in the way of urban progression. This progression, the minister calls progress. Without trees or storymakers and tellers, the new stories would not guide us into meaning and evolving models of consciousness. We would spiral out of orbit into a chaotic mad world of meaninglessness. Human life would wither. Storytellers continue to serve, as trees and greenery serve the lungs and the human body, without a need for medals and statues and affected reverence. I thank the rare spirits who show their gratitude to the invisible work—those who hug trees and books and are deemed insane. Our words renew visions as oxygen renews the body, allowing humans to re-evaluate our path when needed. Human strength arises from many invisible works which do not receive the limelight of Sunday morning, yet are integral to the smile and the aura of happiness visible in my neighbour who sang and participated in the perpetuation of her favourite story. I know that today as every Sunday, she will return smiling. She smiles and shines renewed for another work week. The song reverberating in her body polishes her cheeks to a sweetest scarlet. She waves and I wave back through the clear window below the blue and red stained-glass picture of a bowl with cherries. On occasion my neighbour has invited me to join her in church, to join her in that glow.

The significance of story in the human cosmos is not a

frivolous matter. The story one believes makes us the person we will become and will shape our actions for life. The story that an entire community advocates, will define, not only the relationship between communities, but also the well-being of non-human beings and the physical planet. It is not surprising, then, that the crows and the ravens cawing and hopping, vying for the finest seats on treetops, eaves and window ledges, appear intent on peeking inside that place of worship. There is a lot at stake for them in those prayers. What happens behind those closed windows dictates the safety and quality of their lives. There was a time on the West Coast of this continent, when these ravens were revered and respected by the indigenous peoples. Now, these birds, alongside those first peoples, are seen as a tolerable nuisance by the conquerors. I understand these birds' interest on Sunday homilies. For centuries now, the birds, too, have been waiting for another change of story.

The last time I sat with obedience and reverence to listen to the stories of Sunday school, I had no hair under my armpits, had not slept naked and only spoke one language. I remember enjoying these biblical stories very much. I remember asking a succession of questions. I remember an exasperated catechist. I was not a *good* child. I did not simply accept things as they were. At that juncture I could have opted for the true political life and began towing the line. Yet, I sought more than compliance and a nod. I wanted to engage. These fantastic stories electrified me, they expanded the horizon of human possibilities, they attempted to explain the unexplainable, they placed demands on what was possible of me beyond constraints of culture, class and history. They suggested a constant wheel of transformation. These Sunday stories loomed large from the perspective of my child's height and my sense of the enormity of the human world. My brain hurt as I attempted to wrap my small hands around the heavy black book, as my thoughts stretched around concepts of sin, immaculate conception, betrayal, forgiveness, love eternal. So, I sharpened my teeth on enduring questions and attempted to bite deeper into the world of meaning. The only spiritual map offered in my childhood pointed to heaven, that lofty place in the Iberian blue at the edge of the sea. The stories aided me in taking risks and challenging my self to deeper understandings. They conditioned and also prepared me. I grew courageous enough, through those stories, to travel into the vaster universe and the black holes hovering beyond the pretty and the blue and toward the true. I grew up wanting to attempt the most daring act: to write my own stories and find my visions, my explorations of what lies beyond the comfortable and the obvious. In my garden of possibilities nothing is rigid or untouchable, the words mimic the oxygen of trees, a gift that will fulfil the shape of everything that welcomes it within. The story gives life.

I grew into adulthood comfortable with not having an answer for everything. This openness allowed my wings to stretch and my spirit to lighten. The absence of easy answers did not lead to a free-fall into an abyss of emptiness; rather it allowed me to float over the bottomless universe of unknowns. I have been perpetually in motion. Mind and heart open, arms stretched, but not nailed to anything, never fully settled; much like this planet, we ride through the cosmos, spinning and spinning, not holding on to anything visible, not holding to any single truth, yet believing, always believing, in the dynamic evolution of basic goodness; a vision worthy of striving for, a dialogue about its moving contours worthy of carrying on.

I understand the appeal in joining one story and joining one community of belief. Be it burning on a pyre, burial in a rectangular hole or being picked to the bone by a scavenger, our destiny is the same; there is solace in knowing I am not alone in this experience. In believing we will meet again, we establish a happy ending that will await us on the other side of this particular story of existence. The happy ending is the conclusion we all crave in any story. A promise of justice, hope and resolution. A promise of meaning. This is why Hollywood has been lucrative beyond measure with its happy endings recipe.

Through the open window that brings me the scent of plum trees in flower and the breath of this warm spring morning, the hymns of the faithful also drift into my home. I savour the sound of a group of people I imagine gazing in one direction, singing with one mind. Moved by the power of one collective voice energizing the neighbourhood air, the crows also join forces and caw with added fervour. Now, the human voices grow stronger, they sound unusually near my window. The congregation walks past, singing and carrying a wooden cross along the street block. It is April.

Jesus was and is important. In a time of anxiety and poverty not everyone can afford a personal trainer, a life and spiritual coach who walks alongside with an answer to every dilemma we may encounter. Portable and inexpensive, Jesus is inside, above and behind me, even when I am lost among billions of other souls. Jesus gives strength when those around the forgotten are too busy to notice who needs a hand, who needs consoling, needs company. Jesus inspires. Then and today Jesus is needed. You do not see the billionaire football star looking at his manager or his agent when he scores an inspired goal. He stares at the heavens, the sky and the real stars. He kneels and blesses himself, and then, only then, will he seek the lens of the camera as Narcissus sought the pond waters for a reflection of his grandiosity.

As a child, I found assurance in listening to repetitive stories that brought consistency to my universe. The first imprint of the text upon my mind became the unadulterated truth. I was quick to point out and correct any misreading of stories that I had memorized and taken to heart; any deviation from the first word brought me anxiety, exposed a crack in the narrative foundation of meaning organizing my world. Cracks are irritating in the quest for perfection. In adulthood, I understood those who find solace in the stories they can repeat by heart. Soothing stories offer a balm of understanding in face of the contradictions and chaotic nature of the universe. When everything in my surroundings has changed except the words, the words anchor me. They quiet the winds of uncertainty, settle the mind that drifts and wants not to be mindful. I understand the irritation many experience when a word is moved. The house of make-believe trembles when I shift the position of a foundational stone to explore what lies beneath. A dangerous engineering feat. The house of belief will shift when indeed enough words have moved. It is a frightening prospect. What can we rely on? What can we trust? And who to trust? Who?

The minister in charge of the arts but not the hearts has also found the miraculous trick across the door of perception. When he repeats a story enough times, he knows it will cement the picture into truth. Just like any bridge in permanent sight over rapid moving waters. For this reason the minister takes to the airwaves, backed by his disciples across the country who phone in for support: in a concerted attempt to sell another budget. He is a best-seller and sells out at every budget. A minister will become popular in the easiest and most reliable way: telling people what they want to hear while planning to do the opposite. This is the oldest trick in the bible of politics.

Children invent invisible friends. Their belief in and reliance on supernatural heroes and their magic powers is universally accepted and understood. This need to create beings and systems that help us cope with a universe we do not fully understand, mitigates and re-frames our anxiety and dependency on another, that other who might be stronger and might control us. This is an inner landscape mostly left to the whims of the imagination and the spiritual needs of each child. Such a child has invoked an environment unavailable in the surrounding reality, demonstrating an inherent wisdom and resourcefulness to cope with the uncertainty of their world. This universe of imagination is tolerated until children are deemed ripe for indoctrination and trained to accept their community's collection of stories and invisible friends; only those and no others. In strengthening the number of members in a community, a community strengths their belief in themselves.

In our psychic need for magic, for superheroes to aid and guide us, we have legitimized into adulthood the existence of invisible friends. By institutionalizing religious systems to validate the existence and perpetuation of these stories, we have lent these characters a serious, flesh-and-bone correlation that we do not demand of the characters populating a child's universe.

I offer stories in the spirit that seeds are offered to the earth. The words will blow in the wind waiting for the sight of a fertile mind. A few stories will fall on the deaf ears of asphalt, trapped in sticky wax and tar, and others will be swept away by rivers and drown. Yet, a few may lie dormant, and others bloom in welcoming minds. In my lifetime, I will know little of what happens to my words, least of all in the infinite run beyond my ears and years. Even if my words survive they will be transformed, layer upon layer, as soil accumulates into a foundation of sustenance. It does not matter whether my grain of dirt is seen and attributed to my name. The words, the stories accomplish their task as they did in my life—by and large invisible and unrecognized. It is the condition of humanity, it is the job of continuity and community.

Did storyteller Jesus, or the tellers of the Jesus story, imagine he would irredeemably transform the shape of this planet by the stories he told? I am not speaking metaphorically here. When he convinced fellow humans they were created in the image of God and not, say, the image of the kingfisher, the daffodil, the h. pylori, the Gatti fungi, he tested our vanity and grandiosity by association with a supreme power. And we failed. We invented a centre to the universe, invented a throne and occupied it with a projection of ourselves. We began to inhabit the centre of creation and encouraged limitless growth and multiplication. The narcissistic human rose from the ashes of fear.

The storyteller set the stage to change the shape of our hills, forests, and rivers; prompted the annihilation of other species to accommodate our unrelenting expansion and our desire for absolute control. When the shape of the human brain changes—by expanding our repertoire of ideas and possibilities, and our location in the complex interdependent map of the universe—the shape of everything those humans touch will also change.

My mother warned that encouraging an open mind establishes a dangerous precedent. According to her, a free mind does not know when and how to stop. It requires external imposed limits. (Think children.) Therefore a storyteller who encourages everyone to expand the possibility of being becomes a dangerous weapon. There are no fences in a creator's universe. Well, there are, mother. Even when the warning words of other creators are not heeded, there are limits to everything and soon enough even the self-absorbed, narcissistic free spirits encounter the walls. The free market advocates discovered their house of cards and we discovered ourselves crushed beneath the heap of someone else's fat. The page contains borders; time sets limits; life expires; the ground shifts, and we call it earthquakes. What is true today is not true tomorrow, yet again may return to prominence some day again. After centuries of conditioning, having learned to follow others who took credit and blame for our actions, it will take time, will and practice to learn to be free. It takes maturity to integrate personal and collective needs, to navigate these competing needs. It takes maturity to assume responsibility for our choices. It takes maturity to be humble and decline omnipotence.

The songs and prayers of the worshipers, returning to the church after their procession, fades behind the mechanic roar of lawn mowers beginning their own version of neighbourhood beautification. I close my window. Sound respects no boundaries.

My vain ego imagines a chorus of people at my live readings, a call-and-response moment where they recite my words back to me. I bask in the unending echo of my thoughts. A shiver of immortality travels up my spine. An entire audience repeats complete paragraphs, sounds out the pearls of wisdom scattered in my works. In my dream, my wordsmith legacy is a treasure chest of unending jewels. Allow me the reverie in this illusion of grandiosity. I dream, as many teenagers dream, of a pedestal to highlight my uniqueness above that of all others, or more precisely, above that of my peers. I long for the elation and adulation of a rock star in concert. I am in awe of the power of belief. Collective faith suffices to bring characters, words, and worlds to existence. This is how powerful belief is. These constructs become more real to me than the empty hand of a beggar at the corner of the luxurious restaurant, the chemically glowing apple on the tree and the garter snake in my vegetable garden. (Why snakes are said to wear garters is a story told in other places of devotion, those not frequented by the entire family.)

It is this song or supplication, repeated decade after century, century after Sunday that I call a prayer. Exaggerate the powers attributed to any Creator and as a consequence my readers may ask me for advice or guidance on matters foreign to my particular area of inspired insight. Followers will trust me to bestow favours, hold me capable to influence the ocean tides and the brightness of stars, lottery numbers and football results. With such wind of faith behind my back I begin to believe that indeed I influence the workings of the universe. I syndicate my ramblings into a Sunday talk show and publish every word I utter. My sneezes, manifestations of the divine voice, are elevated to sacred invocations. I convince you every idea I present encapsulates a hidden message and resonates in mysterious meanings accessible to few. A class of interpreters of the word is born. A class of re-packers of the word follows. They will ensure the correct packaging and delivery of the word.

To the minister on the radio and to the minister on the pulpit at the end of the street, I say: from the regurgitated prayers of my followers I learn nothing of them. In turn, they may not learn anything about themselves. In the rare misfortune I inadvertently become a best-seller god, I will not encourage my followers to blind me with the incandescent power of my own words. I will want to stir the waters, not simply open them to let the one who agreed with me through, only to drown the next, deemed unworthy. I will not be pleased with conformity. I will send followers out the door with more questions than when they arrived. I will promote dissent and autonomy and competing voices. How else will I evolve and mature as a god?

I prefer to inspire. I do not wish to be an idol. I do not believe my life perfect and worthy of repeating. I believe no one's life worthy of repetition to the tee. The inspiration is a spark that lights the way, and you choose to burn the way you want to burn. You are your own torch. Find the many unrecognized flickers of inspiration whether in agreement or difference; find them in your or other communities. At those times you feel lost and empty, I cannot stop you from emulating me. On occasion, it is human to find ourselves lost on the empty stretches and to seek guidance and support. I regret it is also human to choose that dependency as a destination. Most of us benefit from two working legs to aid in building our independence and interdependence. Weakness and laziness also belong to us; however, if I am to grow up and gain autonomy and consciousness, I can be expected to work at lighting up my own ideas in order to illuminate the path. This is the path of the gods. Awareness of others besides ourselves. No surprises will be found when blindly following the footsteps of another; the immortality of ennui will await me.

I will not be the end of the conversation. I will not be the last word. I am a beginning of countless beginnings, I am an ingredient of many interchangeable ingredients. I am not an end or the end. I am not your destination. I do not wish to be your destination. Words carry magic. While not one set of words unlocks every truth at all times, different words exhume distinct truths. The official monopoly on truth represents a dangerous attempt at a monopoly on words, an attempt to control the magic of the word itself, its essence and power to open up different levels of consciousness and experience, its capacity to open new windows in any wall corralling human potential. The capacity of words to create and re-create our universe underpins the necessity to preserve its inherent freedom. The loss of diversity in stories is as dangerous and monolithic as the loss of natural habitat through the disappearance of forests, flowers, finches. The need for undisturbed and diverse natural habitats are needed for the equilibrium of the whole planet. The need for such diversity of natural experiences equals the need for diverse storytelling voices so that our societies can finally rejoice in spiritual, emotional and intellectual diversity and equilibrium.

To the politician on the radio I say, I understand you. You support the stories that reinforce your view of the world and your self-righteous demeanour. Most of us seek safety in certainty, and certainty in numbers. The more people agree with you the more self-righteously you behave. You know a lack of competing and alternative visions facilitates your job of convincing others to follow and obey. You don't have to re-balance and readjust your own understandings. It's much easier to simply impose your blueprint. In the financial world you defend a competitive posture because access to wealth and capital offers certain people of your clan a leg up. In the world of ideas you prefer a totalitarian regime. Ideas are free and one does not require a history of connections and offshore accounts to elaborate a thought. Dangerously egalitarian, ideas require discipline, method, cultivation of an open mind, an investment in education. There is a cost in preparing an athlete of reason to cogitate farther and slower. I understand, dear politician, that you prefer to train professionals who favour drilling holes in the Arctic sea rather than holes in your arguments. They bring us oil and gadgets that propel us extremely far yet not as far as happiness. I understand. Investing in critical thinking, wisdom, logic and insight frustrates the smooth implementation of autocratic governing styles. I understand your priority in dismantling the cultivation of visionary imagination, philosophical thinking, civic inspiration and participation. I don't expect perfection from you, minister. I do expect the humility to accept that you too can err, you cannot alone see the entire picture, and you (like me) require the eyes of your critics to point out your blind spots, your bias, your unconscious, if not hidden, agenda.

The essence of my artistic life places me as an outsider. Allows me distance and perspective. The farther away from the allure of power the less influenced I am. I am the bubble buster. I am still learning to deliver compassion with a poke and a pop. I am not perfect. I am not seeking your blessing. I am content on the periphery. I am the fire tower sentinel who spends a few hours every day removed from the company of others to better detect the destructive strikes in the dense forest, to catch the first smouldering that would turn into a devastating fire were no alert to be issued. I too stand aside from power. Some fires arise because unconscious people do not attend to details, do not understand the wheel of connections and consequences or care not to. Hot coals or discarded cigarettes butts will smoulder like warning whispers that slip past the awareness of most. Before long, the meek and the discarded will rise in a flare and roar, becoming monsters. A fire is not aware it is a monster. By then it is too late. Its essence is to consume and destroy whatever it touches. It feeds itself in a vicious circle, it grows larger and larger as it devours. It grows out of control and knows no limits.

I am also not seeking your iron fist on my neck when I say the minister is lying; when I am an oracle; when I am the thorn in your complacent bed of privilege; when I inspire others to search beyond their self-interest. I understand smart-asses are a pain for those wishing to exert absolute control and dispense privileges to their clans of back-scratching. Power prefers overworked, under-educated citizens, those asleep, tied up, obedient. It requires followers, and it requires early and intensive training to create a worker instead of a citizen. Weekly training if possible, plus tea and cookies, and TV to sweeten the bait.

Artists, the ones not on public payroll, or if in public payroll not following your instructions, are not welcome under your roofs. For that you already have your speech writer and the most popular writer of all, and he is dead. An oral storyteller, Jesus wrote nothing. How convenient. Now you may reshape and rewrite his already mediated meanings in any suitable flavour. This is a reason many writers and artists only become famous after their deaths. Think Darwin, Nietzsche, Marx. They can no longer defend themselves from the pillagers, from the manipulation of their ideas and the shifting of their contexts.

To all ministers of the word, with portfolios or without, with or without pulpits and flocks, I say, I recognize your skill. Houdinis are difficult to pin down. Dressed in charm and snake oil, slipperiness douses your skin and handshake. You have made a career of it. You excel at delivering stories that deceive, mask and deflect the essence of truth. It is a sign of the times that you succeeded with lies and want to silence those whose job aims to peel the masks of deceit. You are in the business of double-speaking with the intent to hide. I am in the art of double-speaking with the intent to reveal.

The faithful return now to their parked cars, their smiles further polished, their suits further wrinkled. My neighbour, as expected, walks past my window and waves. I sit predictably at my window and also wave. It is Sunday and she has found more answers to her questions. It is Sunday, and I have found more questions to my questions. I turn the radio off. Tomorrow is Monday again, and I, am yet to rest.

Victoria / 2006

I, THE JESTER

"It'll piss a lot of writers off, and maybe even you, but I see writers as entertainers more than anything." G. E.

The role of art and artists solely as entertainers is a perception shared by many. The post-WWII war generations raised on technology-driven, mass-distributed entertainment diets may indeed never have experienced alternative forms of cultural delivery and participation, once prevalent in other times and societies. These citizens expect culture to be one more consumer activity in the ever expanding portions and diminishing variety of the consumer menu. This situation benefits the super-sized corporations and their financial bottom lines, including those corporations operating and controlling more of the cultural creation fields. Hollywood and TV standards have, in turn, become the measure of success for many other artistic disciplines competing for attention and economic survival in the cultural market place; notwithstanding alternative creators who continue to raise their works above the cultural pabulum while cognizant of their shrinking audiences as a consequence.

Allow me to add to this distorted picture entertainment sections of newspapers, featuring bite-size paragraphs of cultural reviews—chiefly of popular books and movies—as a mental side-dish to accompany the bacon, hash browns and fried eggs already greasing up that same consumer brain. In many other countries that newspaper section is called *culture* and is devoted to dance, theatre, opera, visual arts, and music; in such countries, people still appreciate sitting down to savour and digest a complex meal, either for their brain or stomach. Need I say more? Yes.

In one dictionary, the word *entertain* means: "To hold the attention of with something amusing or diverting." Now, finally I understand what has been expected of me and what I have failed to deliver in my books as a cultural object and in my book reading performances. The TV-bred generations have grown up expecting me to deliver a good laugh and a good time. In the tradition of the jester, the court's fool, the clown, I am now also expected to be the human factory of laughter and good feelings. All this because corporations have yet to manage assembling a machine with sufficient intelligence and spontaneity to generate original humour on demand.

For the initial five years of my life, fortunate to be born at a time and in a country without TV, I avoided the collective hypnosis of the screen's charm. By the time my parents returned to Portugal, where weekday TV broadcasting occupied less than a handful of hours each evening, I had already experienced growing up without this technological crutch for my child's imagination. I preferred to run in the fields, climb trees, and make up games with friends, over sitting compliantly, entranced by the glow of the black-and-white TV box. When I did sit down, I preferred to actively interact with the object before me, whether it was a book or a Lego construction. I had already experienced plenty of human boredom and had learned to engage my imagination to transform my reality, to shape and control my mental environment and my attitude toward it. I had developed the muscles of my mind in order to lift me over boredom's hills. I learned autonomy, I learned self-directed action, I learned self-responsibility for my mental well-being. I practiced choice.

The screen, a visual sedative, is placed today before children even before they have a choice to say no, even before the symptoms of ennui strike. In the nineteenth century such sedation was provided by the medicines of the time, which likewise provided the all-too-busy parents, struggling for time to crease their endless layers of garments or to polish their pocket watches and cutlery, a tool to control their unreasonable offspring: an array of soothing syrups containing morphine, opium, codeine, or heroin, guaranteed to shush the children's unreasonable demands for undivided attention and love. In today's enlightened times, we have evolved from those archaic sedation methods to a more complete sensory experience when drugging of our children. A slight improvement, a few might admit. It will not take long before the screen reigns as a one-dimensional extension of the children's fingertips. They look up to a wall or they look down at their laps for the audiovisual crumbs of their salvation from ennui. Children don't learn the skills to walk away or to look inside themselves for the answer. The most powerful and invisible prison has been invented.

In the making of culture, before the advent of modern electric and electronic technology, the citizen stood a breath away from the experience of culture and often became a participant, or might I say, a spice present in its live production and delivery. In that lively, human exchange, the citizen represented an essential ingredient in the alchemy of a performance. Not just as a passive audience, either; there was also the possibility of standing up to sing, dance, clap and deliver their instant feedback to the performer who, thus inspired, crescendoed accordingly, and rose to the interaction. Sometimes, when the eggs started flying, the performer relocated the conversation elsewhere. The feedback was always a clear shout away.

Despite efforts to reanimate intimate culture through living-room concerts or cozy cafés, this personal brew of cultural exchange is now fringe. Authentic folk-culture is disappearing, replaced by professionals who deliver their live art and accompanying merchandise from a distance, in arenas and stadiums. In my childhood I encountered little divide between player and participant. I smelled the wine breath and acrid sweat of the culture-maker who sang and played during the corn husking or grape harvest. I remember a time when every family counted someone who could spin a tale by a fireplace, and a few others who played a musical instrument while everyone could sing along by heart to a repertoire of one hundred songs without missing a beat.

Although the book and the gramophone record had already set in motion a divide between the immediate making and the experience of culture, TV and Hollywood screens widened such divide and occupied almost exclusively its space as a cultural experience. Whereas, previously, some households read books or listened to music, now nearly every household in North America owned and gathered around the screen to occupy most of their leisure time. Not only did the speed and synchronized reach of these new audio-visual technologies add extensive, simultaneous exposure and speed to the delivery to audiences, but also an absence of control to the timing and pace of that content delivery. Either the viewer sat before the screen at the moment of broadcast and watched the show or they missed the experience. In addition, no pause was possible, as in pausing the turning of a book page in order to pick the reading up later, the option to reread it at our chosen time in the event we failed to understand something, or want to reflect on a sentence or an experience surfacing.

TV and Hollywood brought us a distant spectacle where one sits in the comfort of one's personal space to become a passive consumer of cultural production. No conversation and little synergy can exist, facing such separation and distance, that fragmentation of space and time. Culture is now a profitable commercial transaction on a mass scale. It is not surprising then that generations of citizens do not understand participatory culture; a culture that requires engagement, exchange and the body placed in the fire of song, dance, play and poetry. Not to mention civic and political participation in the process of governance. Many generations now have never been asked to help shape their reality. Only to consume. They have been well trained in alienation. Choice is reserved for which button I press from the available channel choices. This is the range of the new activism. Cynicism is the weed that proliferates in the impoverished and imbalanced spirit lacking essential nutrients.

Technology has become the body of the new culture. The human body has been removed from the equation; and herein likely resides the seed of resurgence, the recovery or return of the future faces of culture. That space of human sharing. This is the spiritual dimension of culture that machines are not yet capable of replacing. A few still crave live shows where the "collective body" of congregated citizens, listening, responding and savouring the creative genius of a play, concert or dance still remains unequaled, as those intangible tingles of the skin are not mass reproducible. Machines do not yet make eye contact, blow us a kiss with a wink or give us a sweat-tasting embrace after a dance performance. Machines also do not listen to requests from invisible shouts of a live audience or exude perfume mixed with sweat and bad breath as a performer meanders through the seating in a small venue. We still have time to rescue culture.

Obfuscated by the neon shine of technology, sitting in the shadows writing scripts to be delivered by gadgets, the writer, the maker of mythos, is no longer recognized as a valid agent and driving force in the creation of cultural narratives. After several generations bred on a fluffy diet of TV shows—the equivalent to the sliced white bread that also destroys our gut for lack of fiber, moral or otherwise—these recent batches of citizens have no terms of comparison. They equate TV with culture. They experienced no better, unaware the culture in farm yogurts was far more diverse and rich in its taste. The majority of the citizens of this North American continent appear to have lost touch with the many other sides of culture, including the far more complex role writers and their books perform in society.

In that light I understand why I am slotted as a mere entertainer, as perhaps in some circles stand-up comedy or sitcom stands for theatre—I have to credit those talented practitioners who deliver a laugh with extraordinary depth of reach and social commentary, reframing reality with insight.

There was a time when people gathered around the storyteller with the reverence of a spiritual pursuit. In this space of ritual the world was made and remade. Amid the despair of loss and war, the balsam of words taught us hope. Words resurrected the erased past any time the silenced ones needed to be honored. By proposing visionary possibilities and unchaining our minds from the darkness we had grown accustomed to, words lit the pathway to the future where we had only seen darkness. In this cave of narrative, we humans sought understanding of the surrounding world, a place where dreams spark people's minds. So we gathered around bonfires or fireplaces, spellbound by narratives that told us how the world was created or how we came to be on this earth. The words offered explanations to every mystery and unknown. Words said the unsayable. Words pried open our suffering and our oppressions at a time or in a place where no such words were allowed. Words once more offered us strength and raised us to our feet when we believed there was not a drop of strength left in our battered spirits. Words told us who we were and who we might become, if willing to be uncomfortable in the labour of reinventing ourselves. Words brought us the bottom of the ocean before any of us would ever travel there. In words, the traveler encounters no frontiers or guards. From the creation myths to the stories of morality that modeled the ways we wanted to live with each other, storymakers delivered the diversity of narratives that became a range of optional maps to direct the path of our lives. These texts were and are blueprints in constant evolution and renewal, unless they are allowed to rust and stultify for someone else's profit. Examine how churches are continuously forced to reinterpret their sacred and fossilized texts to maintain step with the evolution of our societies; a must, in order for churches to remain relevant as social forces and brokers of political power.

In most of the world outside North America, and until the twentieth century, people also gathered around narratives in order to be inspired, educated, and challenged. That role of the storymaker is the reason writers were revered for their insight, their ability to see in and through and beyond. Storymakers were seers willing to tread where few dared. We "reported" on the far edges of the mind, of perception, of invention, of belief. It was a mad but respected pursuit with acknowledged benefits to the community. The price of living at and over the edge has always been high. Loneliness, anxiety and anguish consume many at these far reaches of the mind and addictions are prevalent among the practitioners. Their pain commonly romanticized and emulated in the drunken poet lifestyle. It is no surprise that in North America today the writer is seen still as a mad one. Except that centuries later we are now deemed deranged for occupying our time in a pursuit that bears little chance at making a living, let alone generating material wealth. We are no longer seen as mad with courage. Courage stopped defining us. Only those rare writers who have achieved social recognition and material wealth are paid attention to—and most often not for what they say, rather for how their political capital and bank account fare in the fighting rings of power.

I understand that we, human beings, are tempted to escape the ominous and painful realities before us. We want to be entertained, to divert our minds from atrocities and debilitating worries. Worrisome times have touched us before, and in varied degrees of intensity throughout history—perhaps they can never leave us. Throughout history we return to the same crossroads and contemplate the same choices: do we run away and escape or do we delve into the eye of the storm, the pain and the discomfort of our fears, and find our way through and to the other side? Some artists have always been willing to be at the front lines of change alongside other visionaries and change-makers. Willing to ask the dangerous question, to propose a metamorphosis of being, to challenge the power holder, to inspire us with hope and fresh visions. Willing to name the pain and the fear. On the other hand, we have also always had a plentiful number of artists peddling the drugs of escapism: sweet, syrupy Hollywood fare; sexy heroines like heroin in the veins; video games featuring gratuitous violence; TV prizes if the price is right This social supermarket of addictions is all-powerful with its marketing megaphones and sales tricks. Its tentacles are far-reaching and easily accessible: consume now, pay later. This rich diet is far more appealing than the voice of the visionaries calling us to roll up our sleeves and remake the world as a destination we may never reach. A change that lasts involves a span of generations standing their ground until it becomes an established achievement, a natural right. This work-in-progress requires that generous spirits devote their lives to plant and tend the frail saplings of fruits to come. Their actions and their lives represent gifts to the future. Such artists eschew self-preservation, hedonism, self-absorption, selfishness.

Imagination is in short supply in times of crisis. People cannot imagine themselves otherwise, away from the ruts in which they are trapped. One gift visionary artists do possess is the key to the door of imagination, to reinvent themselves, their communities and the world, particularly in strenuous times.

Education becomes key for our evolution as creatures capable of deep consciousness and insight. Ignorance is our burden. Ignorance dwells within us all. It is easy to detect it in my present if I dare imagine myself in the future, gazing at the rear-view mirror. Centuries from now what will people be saying of our times and our savage, crude, heartless ways? I do this exercise often to face myself before the mirror of the future, to look into the eyes of my own ignorance and lack of understanding. I see into the cultural limitations of my times and its prescribed normalcies. The exercise requires an imaginative leap. It is far easier to gaze back four centuries and see slavery, then twenty centuries deeper and see the brutality of gladiator games and point an easy finger at the savage aspects of their societies.

The casting of the writer as entertainer and modern jester serves the new economic powers dedicated to producing homogeneity and conformity, therefore training workers and not citizens. True cultural citizens question and reflect on their choices to find meaning in their existence. A literature that questions and reflects, that challenges and awakens us to our oppressions, reminds us of the ways we are shortchanging our precious time on this earth. A literature of justice and equality challenges us to listen to the heart and to each other's suffering. It is a literature that requires time, courage and commitment from its readers. It delivers pain before the birth of a new self, not entertainment, laughs and escapism. You have to meet the teller in the eye of discomfort. Just ask any birthing mother eschewing sedatives and climbing the hills of pain before the reward of elation. She is present. She is acutely alive, in pain as in joy. It is the same glass window that invites in the dark night and the glorious day. No shortcuts. A shortcut brings separation from direct experience, and consequent impoverishment.

If I were not willing to adjust to the realities of the market, my friend suggested I consider writing for the masses to make a buck—the sophisticated writer thus condemned to soup kitchens. Or the alternative: better lunch menu choices in academia, I am told. Plus fatter retirement pensions to allow tackling the quirky book projects. For the commercial avenue, my friend offered the example of an artist of success, who decided to film commercials for McDonald's as a way to bring in cash. Now he is generous enough to put bread on other people's table by hiring them—to enhance his profits, too, I presume. This was presented as a reasonable compromise. I suppose it is for those who think ethics is a new tasteless type of meat-substitute for rainforest-raised burgers.

Working for McDonald's or Monsanto comes not without a terrible deal of damage to other people, other living creatures and the planet. Let me just mention destruction of rainforest for cheap meat production, or the workers' conditions and wages in McDonald's fast-food chains faring less than subsistence level. This is a new version of corporately correct slavery ("fast-food chains" carries its own devious poetic irony, doesn't it?). Not to mention the promotion of a diet that poses serious long-term health consequences and social costs for individuals and the fabric of society. I won't even begin to discuss the garbage it generates.

Could I copywrite for Monsanto or McDonald's as a way to feed my children?

I hope I am never placed in a position where I must weigh the question and then sacrifice my moral integrity. I'll go back to washing dishes or waiting on tables of a family-owned restaurant. My children may not enjoy the sweet excesses of contemporary middle class, but they will have a fuller awareness, spirit and empathy, a core integrity to refer to when in need. Models and principles of integrity are our compass to guide us across the murky world of power and greed, whose values reign in every corner of Wall Street and beyond. When it comes to leaving the world a better place, this is what we have lost in the capitalist society: a moral stance.

We have arrived at such a dead-end that it is now

imperative to think beyond ourselves. As long as enough of us say no to selling our values and morals, we will be making important statements to those who look up to us for a measure of the world they are arriving in, for a measure of the world they will carry on to the future. We require a moral stance as individuals and as communities. Communities can only have a moral stance when the individuals who stand up have added up in numbers to be a community. That is why Stalin and Hitler rose to power while millions stood by idle. To think beyond ourselves is urgent.

If the hollowness in the arts, as in our food and moral core, are so dreadful a curse, and if indeed it corrupts, sickens and paralyzes us, why are we gravitating en masse to the consumption of such goods to fuel our minds and bodies? Are we not innately wiser with an instinct to thrive? Unfortunately, we are vulnerable to psychological manipulation, trained to behave in established patterns modeled and imposed by forces greater than the individual. The wholesome view of life has become unfashionable, exiled, abandoned, shunned, ignored, unsupported. At best it resurfaces in a fragmented, out of context and commercialized form as seen in yoga, organic, vegetarian, gluten-free, emotional self-regulation movements.

The conscious, wholesome life requires harder work, longer commitment, slower processes of engagement. The quick fix of a fast-food meal in a burger joint is attractive. I understand the appeal. On occasion, it might even be a reasonable option. It becomes a problem when established as the norm rather than the exception. In addition, beyond the socially addictive power, the fluff contains biologically addictive elements that turn one dependent and forever craving the chemistry of instant pleasure in our veins, minds or stomach: with excessive salt, sugar and fat. That is a reason why our innate wisdom will easily be sabotaged by forces we do not understand and have underestimated. Ask any addict. Ask anyone unable to control their consumption of sugar, porn, pain, nicotine, television, caffeine, video games, pleasure or cocaine. The bodies become servants of a more forceful voice who has taken over body and mind. It is not an equal voice. It is not an equal conversation.

It has come to the point where the consumer does not even understand there is a choice beyond fast entertainment for the mind to quell his intellectual or spiritual hunger. Many attempt to fill it with fluff which could be filled with one serving of a dirt-speckled carrot—er poem. This wholesomeness is rare and becoming rarer in the shelves of the supermarkets of contemporary culture. The vast majority of those raised in North America today will most likely never taste a pear or peach ripened on a tree, let alone entirely local fruits and vegetables. They have nothing with which to compare their experience. They do not even understand what they have lost in nutrients, flavour and texture. Culture itself has become mostly green and unripened in their rush to satisfy the market's addiction to a name or a brand. They feed the marketing machine of more and more in this spectacle of cultural consumption. Books are written with sugar ink, salt and grease coat page after page, gratification never delayed. Keep the anxiety high and the adrenaline rushing with ever present danger, sexual bait and flying fists and bullets. Reader or consumer, we are in continuous state of alert. No one can relax into the depths of pause and contemplation, the deep, slow chewing of the reality around us. That state of mind elicits scrutiny, pondering, evaluation. A pause. Ultimately, a time of choice. Reflection beyond what appears to be. You might see through the high, the illusion, the delusion and stop buying into it. You may stop following the pied piper of commerce.

To place a fast read near a slow, more difficult one and say, "Let the market decide," is to place a cookie beside a slice of seven-grain bread, a cherry pastry beside a dirt-speckled carrot. Let the sugar addict decide? It is not a free choice. The conditioned mind has already decided before the choice was presented. Only information, modeling restraint, explanation and awareness of long-term consequences might open a new lifestyle window, might prevent establishing the dependency in the first place; so that both products might be offered on an equal footing where reason tempers raw, compulsive emotion.

The question is not whether Hollywood frivolity should exist or not. Culture was made magnificent, resilient, and life-inspiring by its great diversity. Before this cultural domination by the superficial, creators could each find their niche and not be extirpated by an imbalance of predators. The advent of globalization and of media technologies now permit molding minds and producing conformity on a mass scale; they sell us products and deliver them to every corner of the world at great speed, exploiting the cheapest sources. This cutthroat economic system permits unfair competition across geographies to annihilate the small artisan. Anything and everything is now outsourced and cheap-sourced by the financial sorcerers.

Alongside small unique vegetable markets with a variety of flavour choices, we have also lost a grand ecosystem of minds, modes of being, thinking, cultural production and expression. The megaphones of concentrated mass media have drowned out the little ones in every field of human activity, placing them in quaint nooks of marginalized interest spread over the nonphysical cyberspace. The claws of competition without rules—under the guise of Free Trade ideologies—have decimated the independent creator in every field. This is true also in the natural world where fauna, flora, and indigenous people, with their arrows and antennae, tales and talons are no match for bulldozers, mines, PR campaigns, briefcases of dollars.

It is generally understood that the artist aspires to reach the widest possible audience. Numbers stand as the measure of success. That could not be further from my truth. I am more fulfilled when loved and respected well by a few than poorly by many. To me it is more important to be understood and appreciated for the beauty and braveness of my words, for the risks and innovation, for striving to speak the truth though it might raise the hackles of discomfort or stir the anger of defense. It is more rewarding to be greatly understood by a few than misread by many—without being forced to adjust the message to cater to the lowest aesthetic palate in a market. One day, when most human beings have the education, the time, the commitment, to engage in a cultural experience that dares to strip them of themselves, perhaps then it will be fine to please the masses. Yet the masses do not usually vote to be led into places of discomfort. They like the buffer of the flock, where it is warmer and safer in the middle. The rise of fear is the dominant and ubiquitous emotion marking the *modus operandi* of our times. This is reflected in the visibly diminished number of people willing to step outside the flock behavior.

My interest in art, as a receiver, peaks when it challenges my areas of comfort with its conscious intent to question an established understanding. Of course, there is also a much more loved and commercially successful aid to artistic creation, which is to deliver comfort. To deliver something I will recognize, to validate my beliefs and make me feel good and perfect, and on top of the world. To reinforce my belief that things are perfect as they are, and they are unchangeable. That, of course, has its place in the artistic menu as long it is not the only and dominant choice, and the only menu.

As a creator, I'll be content with a small, attentive, engaged audience accompanying me to the far edges of my explorations. While that stance as an artist is easy to make, as a breadwinner the choice becomes more intimidating. Too small a community cannot sustain an artist with food, or supplies for my daily explorations of and reports on the world as I perceive it. It requires greater commitment from a larger community to save their artists, just as it requires commitment from a community to save their small farms and forests.

I agree with my friend, I should continue to write and publish, even if it cannot financially provide for my subsistence. I must again return to the pursuit of storytelling from the archaic perspective of it being the oldest unpaid profession in the world, and I will tell my stories without complaints, and remain without the expectations of compensation for my already recognized efforts.

I'll write, but not for Monsanto or McDonald's. I will not write just for easy laughs. Not all laughs are born equal. It is my desire and calling to continue to offer a type of literature that nourishes its transformative impulse by rediscovering the pulse of our concerns after decades buried beneath the layers of fat that confine us to our couches. I will continue to write literature that reclaims the field of novel ideas and thus is deserving of the novel; I'll write for those vanishing citizens who still crave substance to sink their teeth into. You can't do that with chips. All crunch and no bite. By the time this pendulum of triviality exhausts itself in vacuousness and returns to seek lasting nourishment again, I will already be fine dust, and with luck, a memory. Perhaps by then my children can eat the seeds left by my words which have turned themselves into bread and carrots.

My friend is notorious for playing the *agent provocateur*, tossing a grenade into a conversation and tiptoeing to a safe distance, from where he will watch the bloody mess, as people squirm amid their argumentative passions. Touching the controversial issues, being willing to turn every stone with sensitivity, is a trait I value when one is committed to endure the rough ride and willing to learn, and when one is not permeated by cynicism as the core motivation for that act of unsettling. More often than not, a cynic does not have a stake in anything at all and appears to solely enjoy the act of throwing that conversational grenade for the sake of the mayhem. Not unlike those scientists who, choosing a lab experiment, cause pain to other beings, merely for the professional curiosity of seeing how others would react to a new idea ... or probe.

My friend missed the adage that the pen is mightier than the—well, grenade—and before he knew it, the grenade had bounced back. As a response to his provocatory statement, I sent him my first spontaneous thoughts, which have now become the basis of this text.

His candid response to mine moved and surprised me.

He recognized what he confessed as the "idiocy" of his statement, and he re-evaluated his view of writers. In a touching letter, he further revealed key transformative moments in his life brought by Dostoyevsky's *Crime and Punishment*, Steinbeck's *The Grapes of Wrath*, Thoreau and others. These moments of awakening provoked by literature had shaken his core, rattled his complacency and lack of awareness.

My friend had unwittingly renewed my faith in literature with his initial provocation. It is possible, then, that words do change a few small and larger things, even if only one step at a time. Words may not change the entire world with a sweep of the eye upon the page, yet words may change the universe of an individual, both in the instance of turning a book's last page, or cumulatively, over time. Words shift our perceptions, shine a brighter light into corners we have walked by every day without pausing for proper attention.

And so perhaps it is incumbent upon us writers, despite the times being so hostile to our highest calling and standards, to continue to speak up for the integrity of a type of literature now out of vogue: a literature of transformation. A literature more indispensable than ever, as the rarified and polluted air of modernity demonstrates. Both mind and body struggle for the return of cleaner skies and water, for nutritious words and ideas, so one day we will regain the sanity of a nourishing and fulfilling existence. And when that day arrives we, writer or citizen, shall dare to thrive, not merely survive.

Victoria / 2014

A DREAM INTERRUPTED

> What kind of beast would turn its life into words?
> — Adrienne Rich, *Twenty One Love Poems*

For a decade, propelled by a faith, a desire, to climb the peak of golden words and dwell that much nearer to all heavens and hells, I dreamed. For that eternity, undeterred by the reality of the icy and slippery climb, I stubbornly persisted in pursuing my dream of writing literature and nourishing the carnal engine with the fruits of those efforts. This fever and madness have endured despite the intermittent red signs warning every fool of the journey's dangers and futility.

In comparison, climbing Sargamantha appears to be a fleeting, simpler prospect, even after history reminds climbers only a third of those attempting the ascent will reach their destination. A few will fall off this summit of attention while still euphoric and celebrating the heights, yet others will vanish on their descent. The journey to literary success proves far more perilous and prolonged than a Himalayan climb. I suspect no more than two percent of those writing for publication reach the summit and secure the view from the clouds.

More financially responsible friends in the profession

opted for the alternate and predictable gondola ride of academic institutionalization in exchange for the promise of a regular pay cheque and assured proximity to books and words. If lucky, they would jackpot a spare day and an empty mind to attend to their favourite child, their writing, bestow it with their undivided time and attention. A decade later they have earned their houses, RRSPs, and pensions. They were bush-savvy in the merciless and unpredictable wilds of letters.

Many authors are overworked and exhausted, multitasking to remain above water and resist the downward gravity of bills shackling their ankles. Our readers are also distracted by escapist cultural alternatives far easier to access and consume. Those require less energy and time than a complex book which cannot be read on the go and demands as much attention as a sleeve-pulling child we don't make time for. Attentive reading is also not conducive to multitasking. Slowness has been run over by speed. This places literary books at a significant disadvantage in the present socio-cultural climate. Perhaps the future of our narrative creations will take the repackaged form of a video game or an action-injected movie. Expect more gratuitous violence to resolve conflicts and overcome obstacles; expect the edge of anxiety in narratives pushed farther so as to awaken the desensitized senses callused from overstimulation. The medium, of course, will impose its rules on the content. Twitter-length novels will arrive to a device near you, ladies and gentlemen. Welcome to the future of ultra-simple narratives to confirm the existing consensual reality and power structures. Give us a pill and tell us it's a meal. It has the hollow musical ring of a commercial, doesn't it? Feed and distract the worker bees with addictive morsels of indoctrination to clutter their thoughts. Scramble their sense of higher destinations and purpose with a bombardment of electronic gadgets and the waves they spew. The strategy has already succeeded in degenerating our bodies. We can hardly move around to help ourselves, least of all to find the clarity of mind to initiate revolution or even a change of direction.

I, as well as most artists, suffer from a socially unrecognized addiction. As a writer I suffer from an uncontrolled compulsion to gather and reshape words in an endless game of alchemy. I ingest, digest and regurgitate verbs, tinker with grammar, imagine new universes, create beauty and ugliness, often on the same page. My social inclusion in my neighbourhood will depend on receiving an accurate diagnosis of my creative condition and obtaining a sanctioned strategy to contain and manage the symptoms, all the while avoiding contaminating the general population.

My introverted tendency, a paramount requirement of the generative process in the solace of my creative mind and cave, turns me and my labour semi-invisible and consequently, only a problem behind closed doors. In solace, I cultivate my independent spirit to follow my own intuition, nurture my natural resistance to follow the easy path and toe the line. My propensity to seek, challenge or create new meanings is an attribute of independence and wildness, and possibly infectious. My autonomy can be a threatening stance to a society dependent on conformity, blind obedience and acquiescence of its citizens to function under the short leash held by a ruling elite.

To mitigate a writer's addiction to letters from further degenerating into a visible and wider social problem, clogging the easy flow of commerce on malls and city streets, I advocate a policy of providing frequent access to paper and ink, of feeding and clothing me to ensure I remain out of trouble and out of sight. These measures will provide me with unstressed time to focus on my daily fix and distraction of words and stop annoying politicians with articulate demands for fair working and market conditions, for support of local culture and creators amid global cutthroat economic forces, or better, also prevent other writers and journalists from annoying politicians with incisive exposés of their double dipping, colluding interests and corporate welfare at the expense of our public coffers with money to subsidize corporations but not culture. Yet, politicians do not seem to believe that such domestication of writers would keep us all off their heels. They might be right.

My compulsive creative condition appears to be incompatible with a marketplace that increasingly expects free content and free culture, while I, stubborn, appear unable to succeed in convincing others I offer a worthwhile service, when citizens can simply download and steal it. Internet stealing continues to be a socially sanctioned and a financially tempting option for many. To exacerbate matters, I continue to create culture even when our works have moved from the already dire cliff edge of not being properly compensated, to now, being outright stolen in cyberspace. In many countries, including the UK and Canada, writers' incomes have plummeted by a third or more over the past five years. According to a 2014 Guardian newspaper feature professional writers' incomes in the UK are now £11,000 when the national minimum income standard is £16,500. On average, for example, a Canadian writer used to earn between $18,000 and $22,000 per year from his or her writing, according to Statistics Canada. In 2005, about 3,000 Canadian authors, or 11 per cent of the 27,500 people who identified themselves as either self-employed or salaried writers, already reported no earnings at all from their writing. In 2006, almost 40 per cent of freelance writers for magazines earned less than $10,000. At present the situation has rapidly worsened.

Our insistence that we do not have a compulsive problem and seem incapable of running away from the universe of letters and jumbled words, despite the clear message it is destructive to our health, wealth, families and future survival, places writers in the circular quagmire of addictions. Our naïve belief that if only we were given more creative time to inject more or sharper words onto the page, we would eventually and miraculously cross that ephemeral line of recognition and be appropriately compensated, demonstrates the ultimate denial of addicts asking for a renegotiated engagement with the substance of abuse or for second chances. The truth is that we are unable to stay away from words. We survive on visions and posthumous fumes of a faith that most others cannot fathom; even to those sharing our bed pillows.

I thread the fine line of madness. I hear voices, carry invisible friends in the soundproof chambers of my mind, I talk and argue with them; I create intricate narratives of magic and dread, unthinkable universes, believe them real and convince others they also exist. I am sufficiently self-important to believe others want to meet these invented friends and visit these worlds in my mind. I share pains, torments, fears and ecstasies transformed into tales, poems and philosophies. I believe I deserve to be listened to and, why not, even adored. There is not a small dosage of arrogance and entitlement in this.

To others with visions and voices in their heads like me, with horrors and injuries in their histories, yet less wise to the behavioral expectations of the reasoning world and lacking the alibi of paper and pen, canvas and brush, guitar and strings in hand, the madhouse or the streets are a certain destination. They have neglected to generate an alibi in reams of paper under their arms, justifying the purpose and reasonableness of our madness. Or they are perhaps unaware that madness with creative intent is glamourized and, therefore, accommodated; madness without artistic intent is ostracized or criminalized.

Professional health workers might diagnose the street population with hallucinations of grandeur, maladaptation, mental illness, delirious irrationality, substance abuse, religious-like fervor, all without an aim and object. Those people also share my need to contribute, my hunger for attention and understanding, for belonging, for love and appreciation, except I am sufficiently disciplined in my undeterred, irrational belief in an audience for my words to follow the established channels and circuitous games of publishing. I wait in silence, having learned to contain my invisibility and suffering through years of disappointment and rejection. Authors drink and numb the pain with the same substances as the street addicts and drunks. We do it behind curtains and inside closets. Mostly. Our deep list of litanies and ailments runs parallel to the Grand Canyon. I cannot help but shuffle words around on a page and never find a just-right positioning. I accumulate words on shelves, words I will never read, yet believe I shall one day. I abstain from the present; I live in a bubble chasing the golden ideas perpetually floating away.

I am a writer, therefore hopeful. I believe in the impossible. I envision a future when an author will be provided with in-site clinics where, besides the materials of our craft, we also receive our fix of food and clothes to carry on with our unproductive addictions of making up stories, rhyming words and unlocking truths with the elusive tool of our imagination. I'm told we are entertaining, can speed up or slow down time at will, blow the heaviest worries far, far away into a black hole, never to return. Some citizens appreciate these valiant efforts to make life more bearable while on this twirling piece of rock, skidding through a galaxy without meaning.

As matters stand, I realize that governments are not motivated to provide me with this beneficial social program. I am not prone to petty crime, beyond the youthful phase of pocketing the occasional book. I am not yet a social nuisance arguing with myself in the tulip-decorated public park. I do not yet obstruct small business doorways with my sleeping bag. I am not unkempt and do not aggressively panhandle in tourist zones. Mostly, my family believes in my fantasies and supplies me a bed to avoid the embarrassment of seeing me curled up on a park bench or inside a cash machine foyer, smelling the money but not allowed to touch it. However, all this could change on a dime, in this social slide where a penny no longer exists.

Governments realize that artists will continue to create regardless of the lack of support or work conditions, the obstacles tossed our way, regardless of the neglect, of the exploitation. The less governments do, and the poorer we become, the busier we get. Writers are harmless, quaint fools who entertain even when we mean to complain and protest.

We resemble the industrious bee in a continual back-and-forth across the fields of language, cross-pollinating the words we touch. We generate beauty and awe by transforming language into images and narratives of wonder, flavours of the eccentric. We cannot help ourselves in our quest to create sweetness and spread it on the whole world. We offer you sensorial sparks of delight while nourishing your mind and spirit. As bees, we have been manipulated to give our labour, preferably for free. Many others profit from our effort even when you, my reader, are buying the jar of sweetness from a shelf rather than stealing it from my hive.

An in-site, word-injection program, a soup kitchen charity for artistic creators, would also prevent me from compromising my values in the marketplace and forcing me to sell myself to a university career teaching literature to students who, after twelve years of schooling, still cannot spell. I know, I know. It sounds arrogant. I could focus on the positive and highlight the handful of five amazing students in my fictitious and facetious academic career who made it all worth the premature white hairs. I'll convince myself I made a difference in their lives. I can bury the departmental politics as if compromise until demise never existed, and continue to pretend that I would rather not be writing more, marking less, not politicking at all.

For lack of an in-site, word-injection program or sobering word centre where I could find support to manage my compulsive use of books, indiscriminate ingestion or concocting of words, a great number of us authors have to implicate ourselves in academia, high schools, and lead a double life pretending love for those careers, teaching other people's agendas, outdated inanities, for students who, in most cases, would rather be at the bar or the beach. Make it a beach with a bar, for emphasis. Mostly, I declined the graduate academic route knowing I would damage the students for my lack of teaching passion and skill at faking interest in Jane Austen, or in other authors no one would ever see me read willingly. Teaching would be a means to an end and therefore lack integrity. I would start a class by announcing my truths.

Dear students, I would rather you be the bobbing seal heads in the frothy surf and me in a lounge chair by the ocean. On my lap I would be writing my opus a mere eight feet from the reef's octopus who changes colours at will to camouflage its existence in the shifting foreground. As it is, I must bring you the words of authors I am not passionate about. I must fake my pleonasms. Forgive me. It is a necessity in the drama curriculum of department politics. Bear with me as I bear with you. Let us attempt to make this journey as painless as feasible under the circumstances. The route bears no surprises. Think of it as a transaction: We step onto the moving walkway and sooner or later arrive at convocation as long as all fees have been paid in full. Be warned: The class objectives and the reading lists are not all within our control. In here you learn to write to please, to be approved and graded. Do not despair, not everything is without meaning or life lessons among these sterile walls. Living in perpetual camouflage as a wallflower is excellent training in life and possibly the best skill-learning jewel in this entire program. Pretending will most certainly prepare graduates to succeed in any endeavour undertaken in public life. It will assure them endless promotions in the professional ladder.

Forgive me, I am a writer. I carry a certain *je ne sais quoi* excess of aspirations and nerve. I will just not disappear gently into the quiet night to be buried in a common grave of professions, joining the collateral damage victims of savage policies of economic profit. Speaking up, resisting, protesting is a writer's strength. Allow me to suggest a few more ideas to save me from selling myself instead of my true works. Allow me to give you the opportunity to save your neighbourhood artist with the same enthusiasm as you are striving to save the dolphins, the elephants, the small family farm and the forests.

In conjunction with my in-site, word-injection proposal I suggest a complementary national awareness campaign to save the non-domesticated writer from extinction by establishing wild writing refuges and sanctuaries. The wild writer is nearly extinct. There are few of us left who were not raised in writing farms of creative writing obedience, excelling at flawless writing devoid of passion and madness. A wild sanctuary would allow me to graze on whatever books and flowers would bloom in my surroundings and to dive heart first into any refreshing lake. Offer me the gift of space, a habitat with food to feed myself. I'll choose my intellectual diet, my pace of ruminations. The rest will take care of itself. Writing is not only an assembly line of words to highlight efficiencies, sell goods and fatten bottom lines. It is also a calling and a spiritual pursuit for a few. There is no manual or recipe. The sanctuary will pay for itself. Charge visitors a fee to view the inside of my mind. No *freebees*. Flower of mind pollination is a life-generating task that must be protected.

In line with the popularity of the social consciousness movement growing in an enlightened segment of the population, already purchasing fair trade bananas, chocolate, reed baskets, carpets, and Guatemalan dolls, time has arrived to include me in this equation and start buying Fair Trade books in which authors receive a living wage and no less than forty percent royalties of the purchase cost to the consumer. This would lift us from the three, five or seven percent net of cover we now receive. It would seem a task easy to accomplish in this age of e-books with negligible costs of production and distribution, wouldn't it? Well, no. Not when the fat beast's hunger for growing profit is never satiated.

For the rest of the population resisting prescribed

egalitarian values of social justice, proud of never listening to anyone telling them what to do, let us also promote a social practice of alms for authors, a practice better known in this North American culture as tips. After the last paragraph in a book, a well-placed footnote might inform readers that if they enjoyed their mind's feast, they should consider rewarding the writer with a generous tip to their email address. Author royalties are insufficient to feed the creator, let alone their children. An empathetic reader might feel pity and open the heart and purse accordingly. I also propose this practice for library, second-hand or borrowed books from friends, and from which authors receive no compensation for their labour. Even a twenty-five cent crumb of a tip would reach a long way towards putting together a loaf of bread, and the reader would likely also value feeding the mind that might bring another delight in the next written work; versus being the last creative hurrah of an author.

Of course, this shifts the responsibility of publishers, of sellers and distributors of new and used books, to conduct their activities with financial and human integrity, to be socially accountable in establishing and operating a business model of profit that bypasses the responsibility of looking after their creators and workers. The tipping business model shifts the responsibility to the erratic, capricious moral roulette of the consumer mood du jour. This is capitalism's preferred strategy to mitigate social imbalances. Self-regulation. Another euphemism for avoiding regulation that forces them to share the pie.

These necessary tweaks in the cultural landscape of the writing culture should aid us writers in withstanding the dark economic times brought on by a savage economic system of exploitation that has impoverished and strip-mined many a profession in the name of higher profits for fewer pockets. In this light, my resilient dreams, passions and gifts will endure this storm. Instead of independent writers becoming a footnote in cultural history, we shall see our dream flourish. It has simply paused before we carry on with more determination, defending the human mind and spirit against the hungry ghosts harassing the coexistence and livelihood of so many on this planet.

Victoria / 2014

paulo da costa

LANGUAGE

paulo da costa

THE MUSIC OF TRANSLATION

Each particular text requires that the translator be attuned to its needs. The needs are varied and complex in any transposition from one language, one culture to another. Here I will focus on the exploration of a text's specific musical needs. From the poetic to the technical, and to varying degrees, each text will require assorted scales of attention to facilitate the flow of language. To accomplish this a translator must be an attentive listener and, in addition, competent at hearing the music in the words. What does the text shout, and what does the text murmur? Will the range of notes touch all ears across all cultures? Translation preserves, transforms and invents. Choices are made. The subtle reverberations require ears equal in might to those versed in translating the songs of the trees.

As a writer and poet, I depart from views such that superior texts carry an inherent, coherent rhythm and musicality, ingredients that reinforce the particular excellence of their semantics. An effective translator will embrace a parallel, lucid rhythm in the target language. In my translations, I have not needed to sacrifice meaning in a prose text in order to preserve the underlying musicality.

In translating, I first assess the essence of the work to establish if music—the score—lies at the core of the text as in the case of L=a=n=g=u=a=g=e poetry or rhyme. At times, the primary need of the poem will speak to the obvious choice I must highlight in translation. At other times, when the need for semantic meaning and music are equally married and essential to the experience, such as in a sonnet or other rhyming, I have opted to highlight meaning. In the instance of language poetry, music will take precedence. I see two distinct levels of music in a text. The most apparent is exemplified by rhyme and might be called the beat of the poem while a secondary one, subtle and conducted by punctuation, I will call a poem's cadence. In the following example, alliteration from sibilant sounds is the essence of this poem.

MUSIC III
    for Adriana

Rita Taborda Duarte
translated by paulo da costa

Simply
    scholarly
    from soporiferous sound
    to sonorous silence
Also
    so,
    sharply sage
        is the solar
            clef

MÚSICA III
    À Adriana

Rita Taborda Duarte

Sapientemente
    sempre
    de soporífero som
    a sonoríssimo silêncio.
Assim
    também,
    sustenidamente sábia
            é a clave
              solar

In translating, I value the transposition of the breath alongside the semantics of a text, the word, the cadence, the tempo. I see merit in not reshaping the music of an original text to the rhythm of a target language. Instead, I endeavour to remain true to the distinct music and syntax of the original work. I do not shorten the length of the sentences from the original language because English speech favours sentences significantly shorter than the Portuguese, by this I mean, I do not change the punctuation of a text. Either amputation or prosthesis would change the breath of the sentence, the breath of the book and, as a consequence, the musicality of the text. I am a reader who appreciates the strangeness conveyed in the sound and structure of a foreign text. The strangeness that stays true to the spice and flavour I would expect from a distinct view of the world arriving from another language, voice and culture, and to illustrate this I have included a poem from the Portuguese poet Nuno Júdice.

IMAGEM
Nuno Júdice

O homem que falava sozinho na estação central de munique
que língua falava? Que língua falam os que se perdem assim, nos
corredores das estações de comboio, à noite, quando já nenhum
quiosque vende jornais nem cafés? O homem de
munique não me pediu nada, nem tinha ar de
quem precisasse de alguma coisa, isto é, tinha aquele ar
de quem chegou ao último estado
que é o de quem não precisa nem de si próprio. No entanto,
falou-me: numa língua sem correspondência com linguagem
alguma de entre as possíveis de exprimirem emoção
ou sentimento, limitando-se a uma sequência de sons cuja lógica
a noite contrariava. Perguntar-me-ia se eu compreendia acaso
a sua língua? Ou queria dizer-me o seu nome e de onde vinha
- àquela hora em que não estava nenhum comboio
nem para chegar nem para partir? Se me dissesse isto,
ter-lhe-ia respondido que também eu não esperava ninguém,
nem me despedia de alguém, naquele canto de uma estação
alemã; mas poderia lembrar-lhe que há encontros que só dependem
do acaso, e que não precisam de uma combinação prévia
para se realizarem. - É então que os horóscopos adquirem sentido;
e a própria vida, para além deles, dá um sentido à solidão que empurra
alguém para uma estação deserta, à hora em que já não se compram
jornais nem se tomam cafés, restituindo um resto de alma ao corpo
ausente - o suficiente para que se estabeleça um diálogo, embora
ambos sejamos a sombra do outro. É que, a certas horas da noite,
ninguém pode garantir a sua própria realidade, nem quando outro,
como eu próprio, testemunhou toda a solidão do mundo
arrastada num deambular de frases sem sentido numa estação morta.

IMAGE
Nuno Júdice
translated by paulo da costa

The man who talked to himself in munich's central station
what language did he speak? What language speak those lost like that, on
platforms of train stations, at night, when no
kiosk sells newspapers or coffee? The munich
man asked me for nothing, he didn't even look
as if he needed anything, meaning, he looked

like someone who had arrived at the last stage
the stage of someone who does not even need himself. Although,
he spoke to me: in a tongue not resembling a language
capable of expressing emotion
or feeling, limited to a sequence of sounds whose logic
the night contradicted. Was he asking me if by any chance I understood
his language? Or did he want to tell me his name and where he was from
- at such an hour when no train was
about to arrive or leave? If he had told me this,
I would have told him that I too was waiting for no one,
nor was I saying goodbye to someone, in that corner of a german
station, though I could remind him that some meetings depend only
on chance, not requiring a previous arrangement
to occur. That is when horoscopes acquire meaning,
and life itself, beyond them, lends meaning to the solitude that pushes
someone toward an empty station, at an hour when newspapers
are not bought or coffee drunk, restoring a touch of soul to the absent
body - enough to establish a dialogue, although
both are each other's shadow. Since, at certain hours of the night,
no one can be certain of one's own reality, not even when another,
like myself, witnessed all the loneliness in the world
dragged through senseless meandering sentences in a dead station.

An important aspect of my inspiration to bring texts across languages and cultures is a desire to hear the immense diversity of human approaches to perceiving and singing our inner and outer worlds. Crucial to this cultural interchange is my exposure to the manner in which another culture breathes a language, and by extension, the manner in which it embodies the world, welcoming the musicality of another language, that touch of strangeness, the unusual, almost rough friction in my ear. What might sound odd to my ear in translation might be a translator's choice to stay true to the music of the original text, the synergy of unusual meaning and music to deliver the exquisite.

It is common to hear a literary work described negatively, "It sounds like a translation." Implied is the statement that the work does not sound English, by extension does not sound *right* and meet the expectations of the reader. To insist on a musical translation that appeases the ears of the target tongue might be akin to arguing that we live in the land of rock or blues or jazz and therefore should experience the songs of another culture translated or adapted to the cadence and tempo of a blues or jazz beat, and justifying such a rationale by claiming it is a familiar resonance in our culture and therefore better understood and assimilated. *Fado*, Chinese opera, *kirtan*, Mongolian throat singing and *soukous* might sound strange to many a North American auditory palate, but does that mean we should adapt them to our familiar Western sounds, spanning from jazz to rock, and listen to the words in a Chinese opera coated in the shell of a jazz tempo and fail to experience the breath and breadth of the Chinese opera? I would hope not. In the same way, I find it unpalatable to dub a movie into a target language since I lose the authenticity, the uniqueness of the actor's voice in the original language, a sound connected to moving bodies and spirit. When I lose the actor's identity I lose the sound of the language itself, language expressed in the crystallized uniqueness of that voice. In a similar vein, it is inconceivable to accept a translation that has adapted the meanings and ideas of a work to our own cultural norm in order to make them more palatable to our values, simply because that would be more digestible to me. The intervention may be with the best of intentions, but it still patronizes and controls the change it pretends to introduce me to. Why then do we accept and even expect works in translation to mimic the flow of English? Yes, in North America we have no time for a *rāga*, a song that lasts from thirty minutes to hours. Is a five-minute *rāga* still a *rāga*?

As a quick aside going from a concept to the concreteness of the body, and for those of us who understand the world best through their taste buds and stomach, I add this analogy. When I want to offer the authenticity of Szechuan cuisine, I need not diminish its fire and richness for it to be better digested by a North American audience accustomed to blander culinary customs. It is my responsibility to meet and experience the Szechuan cuisine as is. Were the cuisine to change itself to please me it would then become something else, perhaps the hyphenated American-Szechuan hot pot or *mapo doufu*. In my case I am not interested in receiving a diminished adaptation of the experience of the spices and fire that distinguish such a cuisine.

Change is on the horizon. The once considered lesser children of the English language, the English of the economic or social fringes, such as Cockney, or the colourful language of the racial fringes of the British empire, from Jamaica to India, the speech patterns of these *englishes* are now accepted in English literary works and are published more frequently. These pidgin, creole, Caribbean or First People speakers have infused the conquering language with new rhythms and influences, and as their social and political visibility surfaces, the English literary canons have accommodated and acknowledged their existence, represented the differences and begun to accept their equal value.

My impulse to bring works across cultures reflects an instinct to challenge myself and the reader. I read works in translation because I seek a challenge, an opportunity to be removed from my cultural habituations, patterns invisible and made visible again by a momentary standing-to-the-side. The degree to which a translator wants to challenge the reader to join him or her in a new landscape, or a new experience, will likely rest on a mixture of tolerance to the risk of losing a segment of readers unwilling to rise to the challenge and the publishing house's tolerance to financial risk. Most people appear only willing to engage with the world, art and each other while expending the least possible effort on that engagement. A growing number of arts and cultural producers settle to cater to the lowest common denominator. At present, the final translation will likely reflect as its determining factor commercial parameters, even if they are internalized by the translator as the value of accessibility to the reader, to the market. Providing something readable. Not that the other options would be unreadable. Not that the market might not be hungry for fresh approaches. The market is fed by those who have decided on their behalf what they need, the market has shaped their needs, and that is all that is available. Not unlike cattle in a pen choosing their preferences from the meagre selection placed at their disposal.

The preservation of the accent carried from an original text when it arrives in the target tongue is not only tolerable but perhaps even welcome. We must examine the reason for having favoured a certain standard of sound over another, which was the acceptance of a diminished range of the inherent music and rhythm of speech. I suggest it is not necessary to blend in to be accepted. These immigrant texts do not want to be diluted and disappear into the defined stream of a national or imperial literature; they want to meet the new culture as equals with their uniqueness contributing to the range of human cultural existence. I see no necessity to erase differences and the inherent separateness. What is different is not odd. To judge something as odd reflects the position of power and hierarchy imposed by those in a position to judge. I prefer to say that an accent, a text dressed in another language is accepted because it is unique and authentic to the person carrying it. Why would it be important to disguise the origin of a text or the origin of a person? The accent provides further insight into the relationship or situation when we are able to locate the *context* of a person we hear, with whom we converse. It facilitates a more complex understanding of the journey across borders, the experience of communication and ultimately, the experience of meeting the other.

New Denver / 2005

TRANSLATING TEXT, TRANSLATING SELF

Imagine me before a mirror, in conversation, in argument. I might be requesting clarification over the intent of a word, or I may be arguing over the most accurate word to express my experience across two languages *face à face* in my mind. This image might elicit a suspicion of insanity for the unaware observer. On the other hand, for those of a more benevolent bent, it might appear as an act of ultimate contortion: mental yoga. This process carries its rewards and pitfalls. The back-and-forth shuttling of the languages inside my mind is not free from collisions and inadvertent collusions. The separateness is not achieved with ease. At times the mingling of words might prove beneficial.

Translating myself offers a second opportunity to strengthen the source text, a text that in itself already reflects an existing translation, the translation of my imagination and my emotions, of my thoughts and images into the medium of words.

The linguistic translation into either Portuguese or English, the second translation, establishes a feedback loop to that self who translated the world of my senses. It tests the effectiveness of the initial text in relation to its precision, it weighs the accuracy of its words, it sharpens the focus of its images. The translation reignites a dialogue and prompts me to return to my original text in order to polish an image or encourage the further ripening of a green thought. I return in order to sharpen the translation of my reasoning, of my senses and, in the end, deliver a creative work that is true to my intent. As a translator of my own work, I am compelled to become a more attentive writer, challenged to improve my communication skills, and I gain a second pair of eyes with which to touch the page from a renewed perspective.

The process of translation unveils existing gaps in a source text; its inherent x-ray view of the structure exposes, if existent, an inadequately built foundation or the hasty finishing-up touches in the edifice of words. There is no more attentive reader of an author's work than a translator's magnifying eye travelling with deliberate attention over the pages. This committed engagement begins with a sense of respectful responsibility, one who holds in their hand the voice of another and embraces the task of transporting that voice in its integrity to another context, another tongue. As a translator I speak on behalf of another and therefore I must without doubt understand this other as I endeavour to deliver an effective translation. I must understand the varied implications of a single word; otherwise a paragraph may weigh on my shoulders and generate apprehension, if not paralyzing anxiety. Unburdened by such apprehensions, a leisurely reader may travel the landscape of a text without the weight of responsibility, perhaps such a reader even assumes the reading journey from his or her own presumed biases, a journey not unlike daily life filled with slips into misunderstanding.

In the process of translating myself, I enter a collaborative process of creation that affects and always transforms the source text. There is freedom and equality in this interaction. My attempt to understand and convey the original text elicits changes. Unlike the more common author-translator relationship that is unidirectional, my interactive experience travels a two-way street.

I believe there is an inherent acceptance of the fact that

no translator can possibly speak on behalf of another without missing or adding variables to the equation of understanding: therefore approximation is a condition of engagement. This framework of acceptance propagates the tension and distance, caution and mistrust that remain embedded in the relationship. In translating myself, trust is inherent. I cannot betray myself without being aware of the trespass, and the weight of responsibility, the fear of not meeting expectations dissolves.

Since a translator must understand a writer in full to speak on their behalf, the task is condemned to fall short. Not because translators are particularly inept at understanding language, but because not even authors understand the whole range of possibilities contained in a text. That is the poetry of language, that is to say: the mystery. The resonance of our words is limitless. It is an echo without end, an echo that moves along the corridor of centuries and bounces in unique angles off the shifting texture of evolving cultures and shifting times. One cannot understand a person who fails to understand the sum of the self. And no person understands the self entirely. Perhaps living is a journey to discover the depths of who we are, breath by breath.

The dance of approximation expresses the condition of the engagement in translation; its shortcomings or the essence of its beauty depends on the outlook and expectations of the reader. If the impossibility of a complete meeting is accepted, then the dance of un-meeting becomes the essence of the experience. It is as it should be. I accept the impossibility of translating myself in full. As the words change shape and sound in the journey from one language to another, as the fluid ground shifts, the space between the call and response of the interaction embodies the essence I seek to create: a third entity. The marriage of the original text and translator, this marriage of two languages will contain a piece of both, a piece adopting resemblances to the progenitors, yet unique in itself.

Translating myself offers an opportunity to strengthen the

translation of self and become a more attentive and accomplished writer.

New Denver / 2005

THE SHADOW OF "POLITE"

At a public reading, Xi Chuan, a visiting Chinese poet to Vancouver Island, stated that after his first weeks in our city of Victoria he felt disconcerted by the quiet. After a time, he began to appreciate the politeness of Canadians, and he even vowed to implement this newly acquired awareness once he returned to Beijing; he would begin thanking his city bus drivers. A good thing, he said. An excellent thing, I agree. I can never over-acknowledge the contribution of others to my quality of life and to the health of my society or to acknowledge the presence of the other in my community, even if I do not know their name or social role. During the interactive Q&A, and to my question of what he knew and thought of Canadian poetry and literature preceding his arrival in Canada, as well as to my curiosity on the exposure and impressions of Chinese readers to Canadian literature, Xi Chuan provided a polite, yet long-winded, response. He sidestepped my question and highlighted the importance of South American and African poetry, poetry, he emphasized, which sprung from places of suffering. Since in Canada we live a quiet, comfortable and by and large sedated existence, perhaps Xi Chuan suggested, between the lines, that Canadian poetry was thus irrelevant in the international arena. He reminded the audience that the best poetry arose from places of struggle; literary insights and inspiration relied on the geography of pain.

The majority of our Canadian literature is quiet, quiet by setting and quiet by its effort not to step over real and imagined lines that demarcate the territory of otherness. From the grand granting agencies to the corporate machine of marketing, many sensitive toes line the delicate catwalk, toes we potentially may step on at our peril. The Canadian writer or poet who wants to balance their livelihood with institutional support must watch their gait or else a misstep might offend the bureaucrats guarding our heavenly gate of applications and supplications. We, the poets in this country, tacitly understand that it is bad manners to offend whoever in the quietness of a snowy winter, also feeds at the trough. This social characteristic of Canadian politeness casts an enduring shadow over our literature.

On this west coast island, and in this country, by and large, I live a privileged existence when compared to the majority of the people on this planet. Yet, even in this country, on this island, I would encounter plenty of suffering on the streets of my city, were I to allow my eyes and my heart to pause, allow those images, those lives to touch me and share their stories of pain.

We have sufficient suffering in our Canadian society, a suffering that requires unmasking since the loudness of earphones, the flashing neon of advertisements, the perpetual laugh tracks of TV programs, spread a generous layer of noise and distractions over personal and social wounds. Yet, these technological gimmicks do not fool the seers, those who pierce the loneliness behind shiny and latest gadgets pretending to keep company; technology does not remedy our rushed or isolated lives nor does it mitigate the human longing for connection and community. The unhitched citizens, caught in the unending race to collect the latest model of the latest gadget, or unhitched during the competitive struggle to locate the limited food and shelter supplies within their realm of affordability, these citizens, I find them among the poverty and mental illness groups wandering the streets of many a Canadian city. In our streets, I also see the oppression and poverty of our First Nations peoples. In background, I see the shaved hills, and the raided oceans. The menu of hell carries on, updated instantly on our electronic pocket devices and vices. I see it. You see it. Who dares to speak, of them, of our role in its existence? Who challenges this reality, who documents in a way that will touch our spirits, not just our brains, and incite change? Where have our socially-conscious poets gone?

A European writer once told me. From Canada? Not much happens in your stories. It is all about emptiness and trees and animals, isn't it? Indeed, there does not appear to be much struggle with social, political and philosophical issues of contention in the pages of most of our literary writing. In reality many of our writing schools and teachers will advise students to avoid the political in their writing. As if a non-political stance would be a possibility. One is either politically conscious or unconscious in one's writing, one is either aware that every way of seeing is subjective and carries social and normative repercussions attached to the social weight of the seer, or one closes both eyes and regurgitates and validates the dormant patterns of the society, followed by clichés, and perpetuating the existing power dynamics, cementing the legitimacy of existing powers and social structures, imparting a sense of inevitability and irreversibility. The artist has washed his or her hands of an important artistic role, to reflect by reflection on who we are, by at times proposing where else we might want to go or whom we wish to become and by understanding or honouring this role we challenge the world we live in. Transformative art implies insight, seeing through the masks, to unveil and reveal, it implies the existence of a critical view and awareness of one's role and one's power as a story maker and not simply story (re)teller, maker and creator of worlds and possibilities. In Canada we are fond of another role of the arts, its entertaining and escapist aspect. We escape to the TV, the bar, the bottle, the book, the movie and the wild. The scale has tipped. This escape will carry on until the day we have no place and no will to escape further. At such time, we will have joined the impoverished and oppressed nations of the planet, where people must face the ugliness and decay that surrounds them after decades of not gathering a critical mass and stand up to what must be attended to. As in any imbalance, any disease, any discomfort, what we have turned our attention away, will come to haunt us a thousand fold stronger. In Canada, we are still distracted and escaping. We are busy building. Another way to say we are busy destroying too, destroying what is erased to be replaced by the new. We are discovering the land, read: pillaging the land for resources. We are also redesigning the land, reshaping the rivers, flattening the hills and mapping the new geography of conquest. We are rewriting history. We are racing to the future. We fail to see the now that is squished under our footstep.

Before you, reader, are up in arms, and without necessity have raised your blood pressure by listing many examples of voices, artistic and otherwise, stirring the calm waters of our lakes, those brave voices we do have, please remember—I am being polite here—notwithstanding the rare and punctual exceptions to everything I have said, exceptions are merely that: exceptions. Often invisible. Perhaps it explains our repetitive national gaze to the past, away from now, and perhaps it explains the popularity of historical fiction, emphasizing the heroism of the people who *"struggled"* to colonize and appropriate new land, renaming it in a new country: Canada. The settlers' struggle, of their own making, clashing with the existing peoples, a struggle to adapt to a new landscape with its new language of snow, ice and unfamiliar predators, predators long subdued out of existence in Europe. The struggle to subdue the people, the land and the animals continues in today's maze and impasse of treaty bureaucracy, environmental decimation, animal culling, and it is not being narrated or romanticized. The job of complete annihilation is yet to succeed.

Our endemic Canadian politeness, well-built like the best pressure cooker, also sports its own built-in release mechanism. As a result our Canadian politeness comes loose in parliament, in the hockey arena, in the football fields where the ugliness of combat, clash and aggression attract blood-thirsty spectators in the time-honoured tradition of roman coliseums, cock or bullfight arenas. No, it is not the skill inherent in the spectacle that attracts the spectator. It is the fight, the bruising, the blood, the snapping bone. It is the extent of this physical suffering before the eye that compels me and you to support it by dispensing our attention to the game. In these settings, the bottled-up anger and frustration of our national psyche unravels. It finds a forum of acceptance and we vote and cheer for those parliamentary gladiators of words and we pay for the circus of skates and fists to fight it off on Saturday nights and release our very own oppressive work week. On our behalf, the athletes bleed as soldiers bleed. We expect these warriors to free us from the burdens of day-to-day annoyances and to help us release our accumulated anger. In the private comfort of our couches we will shout, swear and celebrate, we will stand behind faithful, ancient family allegiances to jerseys and emblems, colours and credos. Proud, we will always choose one side of the battle. The righteous one is ours. Always. We don't believe it could be otherwise.

The trouble with the dark side of polite in literature, or in mundane life, rests in the loss of my authenticity. I like to know that the people I interact with will be real with me, and I with them. That I can know them. Reciprocity is the civic password of the polis. I know what makes them boil, why it makes them boil, in the same way that I may know what makes them laugh and sigh and why. I seek courageous words that draw down the veils and articulate the unsayable, I seek those who name what I fear to name. A literature that tiptoes around difficult issues does not offer me a model to navigate past the sticky roads of maple syrup poured at my feet to stop, distract and sedate me into babble, gobbly-gock and perpetual pleasantries. The *baksheesh* poured at my feet in the form of tax refunds, Olympic pride, gold medals, scholarships, grants, championships and prizes, do not tempt me into silence. I look at art rather than politics for inspiration and social change. The legislative bodies prefer rubber stamping the status quo. Most politicians eschew the risk-taking of social and economic innovation, therefore they are not true leaders. Exposed to a forum of varied responses and approaches in civic life, I form my own view. My insights arrive from the inspiration of encountering and reading other people's responses to their life engagement, an accumulation of readings and exchanges, until I arrive at my unique synthesis and perspective and then begin the process again. When I am afraid to offend, I am afraid to engage. When I live in a culture that chooses to avoid the discomfort of differences, which ultimately is the discomfort of distance and separateness, and does not provide and foster respectful forums where arguments coexist and challenge perception in the house of countless-shaped mirrors, then I live a muffled existence. A life in the arid lands of the mind is a life in the fourth world, minus the sun, the postcard beaches and the dynamic culture. A society that avoids the outspoken, shows no desire in knowing what we think about anything and everything, I live in a disengaged culture. A cultural void. In the end, a disengaged culture reflects a culture of fear. A culture of fear is small and retracted, and in no way can it possibly affect others, affect the course of events by participating in the discussion or the action. It is a culture packed and sealed away in a pretty yogurt container, the goodness and potential badness have been pulverized, that is to say, pasteurized. Next, the culture is reengineered, the lost ingredients selected with care for desired traits, recreated in vitro—that is to say, a controlled environment. It is a controlled culture, no surprises there. Now, place a pretty designer label and call it live culture again. Indeed, examine our plastic foods as a reflection of the lack of vitality in our human organic and cultural systems.

More and more, our writing reflects the political theatre of our nation. Behind the culture of politeness, a culture of distrust conducts the affairs of our Canada and the relationship between citizens. I understand that in any given interaction I do not receive, nor am I offered, the genuine representation of the other. Friend or not, we are enveloped in a mirror of manufactured distortions. I can never relax to the understanding of knowing where things stand, and as a consequence, trust to act in accordance. When I know the truth, I can make an informed choice about my role in the engagement. If I do not know, I am deceived. Are we writers speaking the truth as we see it? Are we afraid? Is self-preservation our priority? The dictator must not be offended. We know a dictator is easily offended in their quest for absolute control over their will. Difference must be quelled and erased. Except difference is not separateness or alienation, not even rebellion; separateness can simply be autonomy; the autonomy to move closer and away at will, to chose one's path or not be pigeonholed. One who caters to the approval of the majority, one who feeds from the troughs of power cannot be bold. Addicted to the handouts of power and preservation of status, visionary and courageous writers or politicians are more endangered than the glimmering pearl inside the oyster shell. The successful politician of our age speaks the castrated language of polls and focus groups in order to avoid offending the least number of voters. The commercially successful writer of our ages, bowing to please and give the market what it wants, bows to the lowest common denominator to please the most buyers it can possibly net. Antiseptic words result for both.

This sea of disengagement touches literature and engenders a cacophony of voices that lack energy, fervour, belief, and in lacking consequence, their voices wither into irrelevance. If I do not write about something that pulls the strings of my heart and makes the music of words, no one will be interested in hearing what I have to say... the writing will be distant, dull and irrelevant. Children keep me honest. They grow bored in the presence of inanities or lies, in the presence of stories restrained and contained, stories that circle and circle, stories that approach what matters yet never touch the fire. A child will ask me to speak of the forbidden, that mysterious and enormous world they and we seek to understand. They will ask me to be genuine and, "What happens next?" They have no time to waste in diffusing, confusing or muddling up information. In all likelihood a reason for their lack of interest in running for political office. Later, punished for speaking the truth in face of prepotent adult behaviour and unequal power dynamics, many children will learn to lie with expertise and will excel at manipulation, knitting their words in a maze of diffusing rubbish. They will collect followers. By the time they enter adolescence, the lies have trained them well. Soon, they will be seasoned to enter our political and corporate business life. They will join the ranks of word doctors, the new magicians of power in this age of persuasion and manipulation.

Politeness is a pleasant trait to foster, do not misunderstand me. Politeness is not a positive trait at all times or under every circumstance. Politeness is a handicap when it becomes a religion and identity. Our literature reflects the comfortable and innocuous middle class lives of comfort, the packaged and canned foods and culture that generate it. Our literature reflects the lack of muscle of our own imagination to transcend the socially induced trance of domestication orchestrated to serve social and economic agendas of cutthroat profit. Our literature reflects the monopoly of the middle class on this art form. I find a mirror of myself in our literary pages, of our concerns, our limited views. Do I believe it could be no other way, or do I believe I can reinvent and rescue ourselves in the process? I do. Do you?

I choose not to be silent, to wear a polite grin, while wearing the putrid mask of politeness in face of a conversation that generates discomfort. Caught in a situation that pulls my strings, I will not leave the strings tense and silent before they snap; nor is my choice to engage with another in a fistfight arena of sports and politics or personal attacks where the point is to win and demolish the other and prove myself righteous by force. The most poignant literature leaves me with new questions to ponder. The poignant criticism aims to improve and encourage others to become stronger, more complete, deeper seers. The challenger is a gift. They open a new crack on my perception, not by force but by wit and skill and invite me to contemplate again, to ponder and re-evaluate what I believe. How else could I grow and change if I were not willing to question what I believe and if I were not to shed old skins?

In this quiet disengagement that plagues the fabric of social and artistic life in Canada, beneath this quiet, I encounter the pervasive issue of self-censorship. I do not require a government, an authority, to impose rules of appropriateness on speech. I have internalized the rules to such a profound degree that I have already chosen not to step into dangerous territory. The trouble, the discomfort is too great for me to step over the line. When someone in the audience predictably asked Xi Chuan to comment on issues of censorship in China, the visiting poet reminded the audience that strategies can be created to circumvent the barriers imposed by any totalitarian system; however, he considered more perilous the moment when external censorship became internalized and the poet automatically avoided certain territories, understanding in advance the forbidden. I wonder if after his short months in Canada he had already observed that we the people, we the artists of Canada are far more buried in the sticky and sweet traps of self-censorship than we would like to acknowledge. The possibilities to offend are infinite. Even silence can be offensive. There is no safe haven.

This is why people and cultures from South America, Africa, and from every other place where culture is asphyxiated by social and political inequalities, repression and torture, have turned to poetry and song to articulate their longings. The spaciousness of the poetic art form allows poets and readers to evade the literal minds of the bureaucrats, and amid those broken lines, those broken bones of grammar and meaning, the poet and the reader find a place to converse between the lines. Poetry is necessary to counteract spiritual and civic disinformation and re-engage us with the authentic, a meaningful language in our personal and civic lives. Is the poetry written in and around Canada, in and around definitions of Canadianness engaging us?

This is our opportunity to answer the visiting poet Xi Chuan. The pen is in our hand now.

Victoria / 2009

paulo da costa

WRITING CULTURE

paulo da costa

REVIEWING THE REVIEWER

After reading my collection of short fiction, *The Green and Purple Skin of the World*, one reviewer considered it a "sensual, beautifully written book, favouring imagistic language," although it lacked plot—"not a lot happens"—and, therefore, the book risked being wearisome and boring. By inference, beauty, mood, setting, voice, psychological and emotional insights were not "happenings" and appeared to represent a liability of the collection.

Another reviewer deemed the book "emotionally expansive, yet boring"; lacking plot, edge and anxiety to hold him engaged. He concluded by acknowledging that the *different strokes for different folks* adage might apply to my book. It was clear from his review that the subtle, sensual strokes in that book's literary style were not within his repertoire of enjoyment.

The flippant tone permeating that latter review caused me to pause and question the state of book reviewing in Canada. The reviewer had failed to appreciate the touch of beauty, the attention to language or the existence of phenomenological insight. Here was a reviewer who clearly enjoyed edgy friction in his intercourse with literature. No literary *tantra* for him. That would be tedious, unnecessary, and he might miss hockey night in Canada with its edge-of-your-seat promise of punches, gore and blood. The furious clichéd pumping and dramatized grunts and screeches of pornography draw a quicker and wider audience too. To the outside, untrained eye, the energetic body at play between tantric lovers offers the impression that nothing is happening. This high attunement to vibrational currents falls within the realm of the intangible for the blunt human eye. *Tantra* requires a profound quieting down. The communication grows deeper when one is wholly present. Watch for an hour a bare, live electric wire transporting current and dare tell me nothing is happening. Then connect and touch it and have your mind and body blown a few feet in the air. *Tantra* requires participation and deep engagement. It is not a spectator sport.

By literary social convention, the reviewer is permitted to say with impunity whatever the mind concocts, sometimes to do so with the flippancy of those inebriated by a pedestal of influence, an old snare for the unwise gods of unripe judgment. The wisest gods understand the responsibility and therefore the impossibility of a final judgment. Misunderstandings abound, even among the gods themselves. Book reviewing would benefit from a system of accountability to deter those tempted by the inebriating heights of a throne from falling into the pitfalls of impertinence.

It is comprehensible and tolerable when a reviewer or reader is humble and either acknowledges their unfulfilled aesthetic proclivities in the reading of the work or their own ontological limitations, not comprehending an experience before them, all the while eschewing the temptation to blame the book. The question of whether limitations may exist in the examiner is rarely examined. What happens when one is missing the nerve endings of the brain or of other appendages, and consequently missing fundamental receptors of information, and in this case, pleasure? Such people will require furious pumping to feel anything of relevance in their groin; subtle caresses will not register over dead zones or calluses.

A book is not a sex worker arriving in a reviewer's lap to offer them a hasty orgasm which they may or may not be able to achieve regardless of the intensity of the *fiction* in their groin. Apparently, certain reviewers require a fair amount to grrrrrrrrrrrrrrrr in their fiction.

I write for an audience who also enjoys the range, from the breath to the breadth of the feather stroke and whisper, where I expect a functioning ability of their sensorial and cognitive faculties. I enjoy exploring and challenging readers to stretch further toward the refinement of human perception and sensitivity.

Many reviewers also appear on a quest to measure and weigh the words in a literary book. They might be the wiser borrowing a poet's glasses and also reading between the lines, to discover those glaring white spaces that resemble a wintry Canada of soft, subtle contours. That mirror upon the bridge of a nose will allow a perspicacious reader to cross to the other side, to the heart of literature where their job is to equally be a witness to the silences. A book invites the reader to the dance between words and silences, to dwell in the space and the length of those proximities. In that space between what is said and what is not said, distinct echoes of meaning arise at each turn of the page. Some readers might call it tension; I don't.

The universe of silence is an endangered experience across every continent on this planet. For the many generations raised in urban areas, the new silence is the electrical hum of wires and domestic appliances, the distant drone of traffic, grown inaudible to their eardrum. I am more likely to encounter a walrus or a polar bear in downtown Toronto, than to cross paths with an under-twenty-year-old without headphones embedded in their ears. How often are we alone with our thoughts or without them altogether? How often are we capable of quieting our mind and listening to the echoes of words we have just received? It is rare to find a person who reads the silence with the fluency of stone angels.

I was surprised my book was presented to a reviewer sharing his potentially influencing views to the literary book-reading population, without the publication having evaluated his aptitude to discern subtleties or insights into the work. A reviewer with equal strengths and experience in studying the landscapes of fiction and poetry would have been better versed to navigate and encounter pleasure in my book of short fiction. After all, you wouldn't present for review a classical flute music album to a professed hard-rock lover simply because it was all about music anyway. Even less wise to present for reviewing an album of classic piano sonatas to a tone-deaf reviewer for his musical insights into the nuances of a work he could not hear, let alone understand.

Imagine an entire concert with instruments played above the 17 khz range. For those unaware of limitations in their auditory range, they might imagine they are listening to an aphonic concert of mindless, jerking people. There will only be silence in that listening mind and the image of a frantic movement of bodies without meaning.

A circumcised brain cannot experience the subtle and exquisite range of nuances in literature. Something has been chopped off. Unless the reader is aware of his limitations, he may believe that what he feels and experiences is all there is to feel. Boredom.

This book review experience reinforced my suspicion that the marketing efforts of small publishers chasing after attention are a treacherous endeavour. If respected print media can deliver ineptitude, imagine the Wild West of the Internet. It also seems unwise to pursue the trails of any willing reviewer without applying engaged discernment and unwittingly increasing the chances of a book being butchered in a dark Internet alley by an embittered, professionally disillusioned writer, turned reviewer for salvation. The practice of casting a review's net too wide becomes disingenuous and brings unintended repercussions to the book itself. The marketing philosophy of *any-publicity-is-good-publicity* attempts to deny the high cost of this bycatch.

Regardless of how many simplistic cheers and hurrahs, positive one-liners and banal, general inanities a book has garnered in the amateur and Internet ring, the committed literature reader takes the din with a grain of salt and gravitates to the reflective, in-depth reviews. The majority of excellent books, although not all, tend to attract high-minded attention.

Bloggers and Internet magazines' attention carries additional pitfalls when engaging amateur literary criticism in the quest for public (mis)recognition of a literary book. When the art of reviewing is inadequately compensated, it attracts those willing to set an industrial turnover pace of reviews to maximize their time. It also attracts those wanting to wet their toes or raise the profile of their name in the competitive literary arena. Most review amateurs are best equipped to offer the level of analysis and review methodology seen in thumbs-up or thumbs-down, without the accompanying arm, shoulder, neck and shall I say, brain. Fast and sweet generalizations do not even involve reading the book with attention.

I recognize that at present, reviewing is a dying art, its quality practitioners going the way of the lathe-and-plaster artisans smearing goop evenly and smoothly. We now buy pre-made sheets of drywall and only plaster the seams for cover-up. The compensation for a review is nominal at best, therefore attracting those with goodwill or self-interest. Reviewing has evolved to become a type of cross-training, a side gig for building and spreading a name for bigger and better things, to build a reputation in another area: say, writing.

Criticism is criticism. Otherwise it would be named extolicism. As an assigned and paid reviewer, I may feel I do not have an exit. I am being compensated to finish the journey and so I will complain, find faults and disappointments because complaining is embedded in the expectation of the engagement. A critic criticizes. It is a preamble to this relationship of complaints and misunderstandings and different angles of experiencing the world.

The reality of the book-reviewing universe reveals a much more common human conundrum. Reviewers face maximum word counts for their thoughts, at times even the expectation of a smart-ass, Don Cherry badmouth; bigmouth tongue-lashing; a populist and entertaining language style for the largest readership. Reviewers are guilty of participating and acquiescing to such rules reshaping the craft. In joining forces, they are expanding and reinforcing the lowball parameters. When there is a job to preserve, one encounters, more often than not, a bluff, a show of bravado to cover up the reviewer's shortcomings. In this country a reviewer is a brand striving for recognition, a name in permanent construction seeking to assert its authority. Apparently forgotten is the high degree of subjectivity in the craft; and instead a reader receives a reviewer's detailed wrestling match with the pages, riddled with attacks, unkind statements, positions to defend—a plethora of arguments that deposit the blame for the unmet expectations, the mismatch of values or predilections, the failure of understanding, squarely on the shoulders of the work.

To bow out of an unfulfilling reading engagement without showing spite or bad-mouthing appears too much to ask of a reviewer—reminiscent of many an embittered partner in a temporary relationship gone sour. It would require a type of humility, sensitivity and sensibility that would have been required in the first place to interact with the words outside their reach. Instead, in one reviewer, I saw a rude and crude, rudimentary argument, lacking finesse, care or depth, and void of refinement. Not all books are bricks or constructed like bricks.

Despite the existence of conventional stories with plot, tension and anxiety, despite a few swift-moving narratives (albeit not in sufficient quantity to satisfy certain reviewers),

The Green and Purple Skin of the World delivered a genre-cross array of texts that annoyed those plot-loving readers. To my surprise, I noticed an obvious gender divide reflected in the literary reviews received. Three women appreciated the book sufficiently and appreciated the range of its moods, voice, narrative styles. The three men, not so much—and one of them not at all. I also noted among reviewers, and in feedback from readers, a curious correspondence to age. The women well past forty appeared to discover more gems and enjoyment in the book's offerings. Is that a sign of life's ripeness bringing a deeper emotional understanding of the nuances and validity of *internal happenings* for delivering insight?

The following excerpts illustrate the range of the women's evaluations. "Da Costa's prose in this story ... verges on poetry and invites rereading for the pleasure of its lyricism." "The tensions of lives in transformation are subtle yet memorable. ... Some of the stories are dark. The tragic injustice in 'Love and Medical Miracles' and the menace lurking in 'My Real Mother Would Never' are mitigated by da Costa's use of first-person point of view shifting from one character and scene to another, and succeed in arousing compassion." "The inevitability of human suffering is portrayed compassionately, and not without moments of humour to balance the tension." Another reviewer, although not praising the book or its lyricism to the extent of the others, still said, "Language acts as a kind of saviour. ... Imagine the beam of a flashlight shining onto a vast landscape. The focus is often so spot-on that many of the stories function almost as proverbs." Yet another woman reader appreciated "a master of virtuosity, switching register, tone, genre from one story to the next. I feel so grateful to have entered his many worlds ... 'An Abundance of Flowers,' a story so wise and so true that its words themselves sing."

Sections in the writings of *Green and Purple* are lyrical, subtle and sensual. In some texts it reads closer to a poetic work, which does not mean there isn't phenomenological insight, alongside the beauty and sensuality in the stories. As a male reviewer said, "These stories don't sharpen a narrative edge; they expand with love of life and risk being boring." Sitting cross-legged in meditation for an hour or an entire day, eyes closed, would also qualify as a bore if what one wanted was to climb a mountain face and generate instant adrenaline. The discipline and focus required to sit for hours at a time, zoning into the quantum energies of mind and body, is not for everybody and demands cultivating a robust level of patience, a slowness that leads to awareness. Patience to reach for the depths in a book is also less sexy. It takes longer to dive deeper and discover the pearl at the bottom. If no pearl, do not despair, for at the bottom you will still discover the exquisite shells and an infinite number of grain-sized wonders.

Both poetry and prose have thrived for centuries without a diet of compulsory plot. I would be curious to know how often these male reviewers indulged in the pleasure of poetry without a purpose. That the most favourable reviews I received were by women is not a coincidence. A gender-acculturation factor appears at play here, as well as a gender-engendered aesthetic leaning, and it sadly underlines the established perception of stereotypes. Though I realized a narrow range of aesthetic values existed in the mainstream culture, I was disturbed to witness this narrowness reinforced, and therefore nurtured, by those reviewers working for specialized book supplements or publications expected to demonstrate a more eclectic cultural breadth of aesthetic views, understandings and appreciation. That the most favourable review arrived from a reviewer who also practices, and therefore, I would suspect is an appreciator of, poetry, is also not a surprise. It confirmed my initial assertion that my book would have been better served by a reviewer versed in both worlds of fiction and poetry. The poetic tone infiltrates the mind and the body slowly, and its meanings take longer to bloom.

At the same time, fortune found me. A new reader who had just attended my Toronto book launch took one of the newspaper reviewers to task and confronted his parochial words in an open letter—a brave and rarely witnessed intervention challenging the final word of established reviewers. Authors have always been at the mercy of reviewers, and an immediate personal response from me would likely have brought accusations of sore-loser syndrome. (This belated essay of mine might still bring those claims anyway.) The author is offered no forum to contextualize and elucidate on the work. The reviewer enjoys the omnipotence of judging a work the public has not yet seen; prospective readers consequently must take the reviewer's words at face value.

This is a privileged work environment that not even court judges enjoy. Only the secret police and torturers swing their fists, toss their grenades, fire their shots and walk away without accountability to their targets. The author is expected to recoil to silence in order not to further irritate the inflamed cerebral lining of the reviewer and exacerbate their annoyance. The author may also cross fingers, clench an amulet and place mitigating offerings at the altar of appeasement, in hope the venom does not spread and damage his reputation. The author refrains from speaking up, aware that in smallish literary Canada the danger of silent reprisal is ever present. The carousel of the habitual friends of friends of friends ends up deciding the fate of your book in a future grant or prize jury, not to mention the reduced future reviewing chances. Small, vicious powers defend their turf with the might of a sword. In this country people take their territories seriously. As the country itself, the territory has to be kept conquered and dominated.

A book review may mimic a type of public stoning without a timely mechanism of counter-argument, defense, or challenge to claims or accusations, regardless of the inaccuracies or ignorance displayed by the reviewer. The book may survive or die on the whims of these people when too few alternate reviews of a book exist. This is a reality for most small literary presses. A small press author is fortunate to receive a handful of reviews, where then judgements may be compared by the reader. Ideally all reviews should flock to a web search repository with reviews displayed side-by-side for the best comparison of the caliber of the instruments used by the reviewer to dissect the book. Then the reviewer is also made bare for evaluation by a potential reader. One sees the world as one is, as Anaïs Nin reminded us. In this case, the comparison between reviewer opinions has integrity because one is comparing their gazes toward the same book. The only variable is the mind of each reviewer. In that light, one male reviewer says of the story "Not Written in Pencil": "The narration here feels affected and forced—'This little incident with Cody tipped her over the punchline'; 'enlightenment is a damn fancy-schmancy destination'—it never sounds authentic."

For two other reviewers' eyes this story stands as their favourite in the collection; the female comments, "The voice here is strong. Authentic. His heartbreak and raw shock is perfectly captured in blue-collar fashion as he tries to explain his current failure with his own dealings with his son. Voice carries this piece." The male reviewer says: "The stories are populated by well-drawn male protagonists, like the mechanic in the standout, 'Not Written in Pencil.'"

A range of interpretations on a book is welcome, necessary and healthy when done with thought, responsibility, knowledge and insight.

The reviewer owns the podium of attention and reaches widely into the ears of readers, *framing* the reading parameters of a book well before a reader set eyes on it. The male, online publication reviewer demonstrated his weak reading skills, along with his malice, by claiming that my story 'Love & Medical Miracles' was a poorly told joke: "Did you hear the one about the kid with that disease and he went to the doctor, and he had an operation, and he was freaking cured? Can you believe that? A miracle!"

This reviewer appears to have missed the core of the story dealing with children's organ trafficking implicating the medical establishment. He applied the anecdote measure to other stories and equally misread their core issues. It is, of course, a reflection on the deductive abilities of the reviewer, who appears to have skimmed the stories. Those stories require an attentive, present and engaged reading. A reviewer presupposes an attentive, present and engaged reader, ideally with a smidgen more sophistication and erudition than the average reader the author is writing to.

One must consider that the *Green and Purple Skin* book resembles a meditation, not an account of a Mike Tyson combat; resembles a type of focus on one's breath, not on the blood spurting from the nose and staining the ring. Most people are not aware of their breath, of which nostril takes in more air or of how deep or shallow their intake. The book requests engagement from the reader to establish the subtle connections. No mushy, fast-food diet for the multi-tasking or distracted mind there. The reader blinks and they risk missing a storyline. I do not bang my fiction readers over the head (or elsewhere) with my pointy pen. I reserve that strategy for essays such as this one. In my fiction I often bring my writing to inhabit the borders of identities, labels, expectations. In the case of *The Green and Purple Skin,* I hang out at that place where poetry and fiction intersect and intersex. That is to say: overlap, trade places and procreate. A bit like the forbidden cross-racial relations that still offend those who defend states of purities.

What to say to a reader or a reviewer trapped in their cultural limitations of what literature can be and lacking interest to travel down alternate roads of experience? Akin to inviting a Western canon reviewer to play a game of *chinlone*, Myanmar's dance/sport akin to Hacky Sack, where the aim is not winning, aggression, anxiety, pressing against hard edges, defeating the other or friction for the sake of friction. Instead, the experience is one of keeping the ball in the air, to strive for beauty, conviviality, the experiencing of sharing and being together and cherishing the skills and accomplishments of each other. Remember, one does not always have to get somewhere, win, acquire or conquer something; one can just chew the fat. Naturally, someone raised on a diet of competitive, aggressive sports such as boxing or rugby cannot even imagine calling the game of hacky sack a sport, let alone appreciating it or playing it. It requires another type of sensibility, sensitivity and breadth of being, a state of understanding achieved with maturity. Literature suffers from similar misunderstandings. My book of stories was twice reviewed side-by-side with another book (although not a repeating title). A wee bit reminiscent of a literary roller-skating derby in laps around the page to see what book would stand up best to the scientific prodding of the reviewer's elbowing and cross-checking. It does not matter if one book was a croissant and the other a scone. Supposedly, the all-conditions-equal scientific trial would reveal a croissant to be flakier despite its many layers and less resilient to roughing up against the boards. Including the cutting board, of course. Indeed—no hard edges on a croissant. No tension for the jaw. That is its nature. Layers and layers of filigree-like dough melt in our mouth. It is rich. Inserting a lab pin into an elephant might not kill the creature, but the same pin on a butterfly just might. The methodology of this trendy evolution in book reviewing, reminiscent of high-school English literature classes, applies a compare-and-contrast yardstick to its victims. My book's relevance was evaluated when compared to other writings deemed edgier. As though that particular book ought to stand ground against a particular angle on a subject, or writing style; or my writing's worth depend on whether it holds ground and a reader's attention in face of that anxiety, gore, violence, to be deemed worthy of a reader's time. As if all readers sought the same experience, as if all readers were equal. A typical monster truck rodeo show spectator might not be interested in watching a nature show on a spider weaving its filigree web, and marveling at its engineering feet.

That reviewer's flippant assessment did not stop at base anecdotes. In his comparative review, his opening and foundational thesis wrapped the two books under a "catholic versus protestant" view of the world. A simplistic, bizarre framework, a clichéd tall order. Shall I say, sanctified order? I must have missed the relevance of such an overarching paint brush. Salvation or lack thereof? Is it even accurate? No. That my book contained three short stories with obvious references to Buddhism, or other stories with incursions into paganism, animism, and New Age spiritualities is not mentioned; as such mention would foil the thesis pinning up the review in the butcher's hook.

I don't make it easy to be slotted, or slaughtered.

Nevertheless, the irony does not escape me when I imagine the absurd set-up created by this essay, insofar as a reviewer may be faced to review this essay on reviewing. And so it goes … the last line never written.

In my books language occupies space. The text elicits attention to its attire, to the style and flair that enhances the shapes underneath that narrative body. The language is not shy. It dresses up to accentuate the contours of that body. It enjoys the attention. No false modesties there. The aim of my language is not to become invisible. Neither is to become forlorn at the centre. It is integral to the multifaceted identity of the text as well as my multilingual roots. No track pants, runners and T-shirt outfit when words are stepping out into the world to make a statement.

To add to many an English-speaking Canadian reviewer's challenge, the stories in that collection are located in Canada and beyond. Their cultural map and fluency expands to reach into four continents. This proves to be a challenge to the insular reader or reviewer who misses background nuances, contexts and resonances. Rudimentary understandings of social, historical and political contexts of those cultures matter and provide a deeper experience. This lack of knowledge means a reader has missed richer flavours undetected by the untrained palate. That is also the task of a learned reviewer: to contextualize and highlight the undercurrents and backgrounds overlooked by the uninformed reader. This requires existing knowledge or a willingness to devote time to research and learn. Time, in a time when there is no willing time. When time is money in a field of little recompense. Alternatively it requires the proper assignment of a reviewer, one who is already familiar with those specific cultural territories in a book.

To complicate matters for those of us with poetic sensibilities in our prose, we are now suffering from advanced Hollywoodification of the narrative form, particularly in novels. Editors expect fast-paced prose and intricate plots, speeding linearly in order to appeal to the short attention span of the readers conditioned by decades of movie and TV industry candy. Movies are where the book's gold can now be mined. The fast pace is required for most commercially successful fiction and easily identified in blockbuster writing. It is said to be cinematic. Cinematic is purported as a desirable trait. No, make it an essential trait. That trait is trumpeted as a sign of excellence in writing. The problem is, it appears to be considered as the supreme trait to create a memorable book. Movies used to take guidance from books. Now, the little brother of myth-making has grown up, flaunts his fast, polished helicopter, pockets spilling over with cash, and with the self-centeredness characteristic of the times, calls the shots of what is true and matters. As in nature, we have now lost the eclectic and necessary diversity in the ecosystems of cultural aesthetics to enjoy a healthy cultural book life.

A diet of excessive sugar, a diet of Hollywood narrative fare is not without consequence. A long-standing consumption of narrative spiked with plot, emphasis in car chases, gun-wielding violence, bad guy, good guy, all within a thick coating of high anxiety, means that a reader will no longer appreciate the natural flavours and subtleties of other narratives. Akin to those who can no longer appreciate the sweetness in a ripened fruit. Their high diet of sugar has long overshot and burnt out their palate. Subtleties don't even register over the dead cells. You need to pump out even more gore-bloodied knuckles to elicit a response from the callous, numbed-out reader.

Both my fiction and poetry tends to cross genres, bend labels, resist pigeonholing, a consequence of my literary work straddling (and meddling) in two languages, and two aesthetic and cultural sensibilities. I often disagree with my editors. I believe English can bear more syntax-bending, longer and more complex sentences, more circular reasoning, without alienating all the English-language readers. Many other languages introduce a plethora of interruptions, eddies in the flow, lateral thinking and side arguments, swirls that may annoy those who desire the business of getting to the point without foreplay. In many other languages there is no simple point when it comes to human affairs of the heart, flesh and spirit. Deep communication is not a transaction. Deep communication is not a destination. It is a cultivation of relationship and knowledge over time and in layers. The strength of English is in its short, simple, direct syntax, which is a reason it has become the language of choice for commerce and pornography, or so is the view of some people. In reality, the truth of the English language dominance owes more to the British and American economic and cultural imperialism than to its own linguistic syntax. Latin's dominance in Roman times was most definitely not due to Latin's own linguistic accessibility or ease of learning.

That is not to say that simplicity is everything English can be. I am determined to persuade the English language gatekeepers that this language of commerce may cultivate more spirit by embracing more lyricism, and bending, and embracing circularity and less efficiency, and increased playfulness, and added beauty, all without feeling it is being corrupted by a foreign infiltrator.

Perhaps one day future readers will realize that those times in literary history when editors asked authors for endless rounds of editing, demanded lean or bare-bones prose, were as dehumanizing as obliging rounder people to replicate the bulimic images of fashion models because it was sexier, it was the aesthetic compulsion of the time. The curves, the padding, the apparently extraneous words and images existed for a purpose. That might also be the reason that padding around the hip bones feels really good in bed when bumping into another, even if outside the contemporary body of aesthetic parameters. Nice padding on a story also communicates additional reverberations, textures and pleasures only enjoyed by those not in a rush and still counting all their nerve endings intact. I do not wish my words to always be lean and dry, lean and mean. Forbidden or not, I like my fresh fruit plump and juicy.

An obstacle to elevating the bar of book reviewing in this country lies in the existing subculture of reviewing. Most people reviewing books in Canada are also writers and not widely read across cultures, languages and geographies. Many are busy reviewing friends' books, busy reading a friend's or their publisher's books for back-cover blurbs, busy reading for book prizes. Generally over-extended and task-reading, greasing the incestuous system of literary Canada with a back-scratching merry-go-round of polite exchanges. That leaves little time or even interest to read an Albanian novelist, a Mozambican poet or a Zimbabwean essayist. We may all be guilty of participating and thus perpetuating this system. I admit my *mea culpa.*

Many a reviewer is a newly pumped-out writer from another creative writing course sprouting up on every campus and eager to make a name, establish rank and keep their brand alive in this ever crowded literary arena of attention; a product of a narrow Anglo-Saxon literature of middle-class, male and white interests and aesthetics enshrined in most required creative writing syllabi. There is inadequate geographical, linguistic, cultural, social-demographic variance in the literary canon of this English-speaking continent. In addition, both civic and academic libraries display a significant deficit of world literature on their shelves. It is not surprising that when a book crosses a reviewer's fingertips and does not fall within the usual Anglo-Saxon spectrum of creative writing class aesthetics, reviewers experience a shock to the system and struggle to contextualize it.

This deficit of expertise and competence in the world of Canadian book reviews diminishes the variety, strength and resilience of our literary ecosystem. After we are finished with the saturated creative writing courses, let us pray for Creative Criticism School to teach readers about the art of reading slowly, widely and deeply. Wouldn't that be a dream for authors, to bring the literary conversation about books up a notch or two?

Perhaps a literary review, much like a genuine *parmigiano* or *champagne* could only be called a review when it has been demonstrated to contain genuine and matured ingredients. Not sawdust for bulking parmesan or CO_2 for fizzling wine in a hurry. In a review we could agree on a minimum standard of half a pound of ripened thought or two thousand words, whichever comes latest. The individual reviews I received varied from 300 to 562 words, or when allowing for the killing of two books with one stone, 500 or 560 words per book. The reviewer who cherished my short-story collection the most also demonstrated care by delivering the lengthiest consideration at 900 words—a telling tally among today's fast bytes of culture.

An acquaintance in another culture, another language, refuses to present reviews with less than fifteen hundred words. He says he only feels he has started to scratch the surface after a thousand. He dismisses the predominance of quickies as unsatisfying for long-term brain sustenance. The Internet forum, albeit ethereal, can bear as much weight and substance as old-fashioned paper and carry 24-carat thoughts, arguments, ideas. A Toronto- and Internet-based magazine published a review of Jacinto Lucas Pires's *The True Actor* by Matthew R. Loney which weighed in at 4500 words. A feast. Coherent, articulate, knowledgeable and intelligent, it inspired me to want to read that book. It rebuked the simplistic reviewing trend recently adopted by others and demonstrated reviewers still exist who care for literature that challenges the reader outside their comfort zone.

Many writers and editors still belong to professional associations that hold their members to standards. However, authors' books are evaluated by anyone who has decided that since they can read, they are qualified and entitled to broadcast their unlearned opinion as a judgement on the worth of a book. That some specialized publications are indulging those voices is another story for another time. Time has again come to entrust the role of literary reviewing in the hands of those who respect the craft of writing and exhibit proof they practice it responsibly, accountable to a professional standard of proficiency and recognition in the field. In this Wild West of Internet standards there is little assurance, for a reader, of a reviewer's pride in holding high standards of thought. It reminds me of the gas and oil industry with their self-regulatory standards trampling those in their path of exploration.

After all, even a babysitter requires a little training to learn basic precepts. Then a reader could begin to distinguish between competent book reviewers and opinionators, and label their efforts or lack thereof accordingly. As opinionators go, we already tolerate their musings and give them unbound latitude in the social media universe parading everyone's off-the-cuff opinions. In this era of individual global broadcasting, any can promenade their paws over the keyboard without needing to engage the mind. The ripening of their thoughts or the taking of responsibility for their words is an exotic concept in this age of *immediacy*.

What to say to a reviewer trapped in the comfort of their

cultural limitations of what engaging literature can be? They do not need to excavate beneath the surface when they operate within the power of a dominant aesthetic which dictates the majority of the available choices in this country. That is why my book represented a kind of little miracle of belief: a publishing house risked the release of a hybrid, atypical book, assured from the start the collection would not stand a chance to run for any popular fiction prize, a nightmare to promote due to its many-headed features, all in a market dominated by the Anglo vein of realism and logic and easy labeling for fast-pitch marketing sales.

The dominance of realism in literature is a scenario favoured throughout the Anglophone world. Its divergence from the lyrical approaches is long standing and more noticeable in Canada, where despite the two official languages and cultures, its cultural wall remains strong and on guard for its own turf. A reason why I cross paths and discover more French Québecois poets and authors at European literary festivals than in my own Western Canada literary landscape. A great divide exists between the two literary cultures of realism and lyricism in this country; not to mention the magical, experimental or imaginative deficit along the same Canadian English literature border.

Also of note, and contributing to the limitation in many of the Canadian English-speaking reviewers in specialized literary publications, is their single-language mind and reading ability. This sole dependency on one linguistic window to the world already sets them at a disadvantage as far as the elasticity and possibilities of a creative language. In other parts of the world people read in two, three and four languages and have learned that strong writing can emerge from every approach. Many Québecois can converse in English (42% in a 2011 census) and I would imagine many of those can read it. Very few Anglophone Canadians can converse in French (8% in a 2011 census). Imagine how many would be capable of reading a book in French, including, I would dare to guess, most reviewers. Let us not underestimate the narrower window on language that monolingualism sets on any linguistic sensibility.

A factor in this decline in review quality is also an increasing disregard toward the book as a medium in the attitude of certain reviewers: missing is the departing premise that the book and author are skilled in their art. Traditionally a manuscript has been selected by an esteemed publisher with a history of standards gracing coast-to-coast bookshelves, and the book preferred to hundreds, if not thousands of other competing works that may remain in the drawer, may remain on the endless carousels of rejections, unless salvaged by the author's own self-publishing initiative. A book released by a traditional publisher has been evaluated by many, before achieving the privilege of being available to readers. An assigned reviewer has the guarantee of a pedestal to his thoughts regardless of the merit of the words to be delivered. Ostensibly their words never miss the mark or, on occasion, would better remain in the drawer as happens to many of us writers collecting a plethora of rejected works. It makes me wonder whether reviews are ever rejected.

Also lost is the premise of delight and wonder in what is to be unveiled to a willing reader offering time and undivided attention to a book. Absent is the premise that those pages might teach one something, even to those who believe they have seen, read and know everything. I suggest a humbler approach to a book, in the vein of a samurai greeting, despite the intended slaughter; say, a little bow. This ritual would go a long way to humble the mind and remind it of an essential point of departure: a state of wonder and wandering. It would lend the task the necessary gravitas. Reviewers appear to forget that many authors are more widely read and more sophisticated than their readers, that not all writers follow dominant culture precepts or writing-school scripts.

I realize that in any courtroom dispensing justice to its citizens, a certain evident question is never posed to the judge. In a time when everyone has become a self-proclaimed judge, time has come to begin to deliver it. Perhaps it is us, the authors, smallish beneath the pulpit of hammer and bible, the ones left with the task of standing up in court to deliver the thorny question. With a bow, awaiting the severity of the sentence, which I without doubt must deserve, I will ask:

Dear sir, is it at all possible, that on the most rare of occasions, despite all of your knowledge arising from twenty years of experience, delivering the most fair of deliberations, and in all of your wisdom, you, my reader and my judger, you may still not be deserving of this particular book?

I therefore beg your reflection on this most uncanny of possibilities.

Victoria / 2013

THE WORD IN SWORD

> "Everybody does have a book
> in them, but in most cases
> that's where it should stay."
> — Christopher Hitchens

At a meeting of writers in which I participated, a speaker apologized for being on a stage where as a writer he was the subject of recognition and distinction, while the audience was separated and kept at a distance. This person expressed his disappointment at the situation, claiming that there should be no distinction between the writers and the public since "everyone can write." The division perpetuated an artificial superiority of the bourgeois artist over the citizen. "We are all equal and there is no need to create this separate writer's class, since any one of you can write and could be on this stage in this capacity."

Aside from the generous intentions of this speaker, to demystify and encourage cultural participation of citizens and self-expression through the arts, his statement raises questions relating to the perception and definition of the arts, in particular the art of writing literature.

I encountered no opportunity to discuss and examine

this issue during that evening meeting, given the large number of stage participants and the time constraints which restricted speakers to five minutes per person. When my turn to speak arrived, three hours later and at the very end of the evening, I faced an inopportune time to revive and delve into the issue that I had been gnawing on. In any case, the concert of yawns in the audience already substantiated the envy of any a cappella hippopotamus-mime-choir. I was also aware that the structure and context of the meeting did not facilitate my potential microscopic intervention over this theme. The audience's flickering eyes, warned of an imminent collective brain outage, and indicated the true direction of the evening: an urgent bed.

The earlier speaker's egalitarian claim opened countless crossroads of intellectual destinations, destinations as diverse as undetermined. Its brevity introduced me to a plethora of possibilities as to its framework, hampering the assessment of its motivations and consequences. However, as a contemporary designer of mind destinations, inventor of facts and maestro of realities through words, and writer engaged in enhancing the contours of fact, such examination is important in order to clarify my present outlook and interpretation of the art and craft of literary writing. That speaker's statement triggered a reaction. It inspired me to ponder and investigate a few of the possible trajectories of such a proposal; it motivated me to rediscover old ideas and find new meanings and implications, thereby renewing my current attitude towards the contemporary texture of the world of letters and the qualitative standard of its literature.

It seems important to investigate the implicit pendulum of attitude that faces art in general and the writing arts in particular. This pendulum ranges from an elitist stance to the opposite posture of utter disregard for the place of art in society.

The elitist attitude is arrogant, and demystifying it is a necessity. Erecting barriers to participating in the creative process, or defending territories of exclusivity and superiority, are indefensible, as they are vestiges of an archaic sense of class with roots in the clergy as the first educated scribes. Such a stance also prevents widespread participation in the dialogue of artistic disciplines and hinders a closer reciprocity between the creator and the aficionado of the arts, regardless of their social class. I deplore the elitist sense that cultivates the image of the writer as superior and privileged, intimate with the divine, living in a dimension reserved for the elect and sanctified, and mysteriously blessed by the magic touch of the muse.

The writing profession does not contain impenetrable secrets. As in other professions, it simply requires individuals engaged in perfecting their art. It requires practicing technique, refining both inspiration and endurance, strengthening a commitment to discipline, to opening the heart and the ears and honing one's critical views. An artistic pursuit rewards individuals interested in cultivating the tenacity and motivation necessary to survive great stretches of the exile inherent in the creative universe of writing. Elitism must be challenged. It alienates everyone involved in this cultural and creative process. It establishes an emotional and psychological moat between the art and the potential lover or appreciator of this art—a gulf which dwarfs the magnitude of the expression, calls into question its effectiveness as an instrument of cultural intervention and, who knows, maybe even threatens the art's very relevance and survival. Elitism assumes the code of execution of the art of writing, its complex literary representations, its secret domains are restricted to the elected, who would hold exclusive keys to its kingdom. All magicians have their skills—also known as techniques. Unfortunately, some zealous practitioners protect these skills, afraid that the charm and fascination over the Art of Telling stories will fade once the traces of its architecture are revealed.

It is important to encourage people to participate in the creative process. Numerous artistic disciplines are potentially within reach of all, were we to invest time and energy in learning their techniques and cultivating the mindset. This does not mean, however, that we all hold the ability to pick up a brush, a keyboard, a chisel and develop a sophisticated opus with artistic merit. As in any craft, the writing arts require skill, perseverance and practice, and a good deal of flair and inspiration. With greater or lesser accuracy and success, time is in charge of ranking those ingredients, distinguishing the mediocre artists from the competent, the respected artists from the immortalized.

Conversely, to reduce the craft of writing to a commonplace pastime, devaluing and dismissing its art, certainly will exacerbate the very contempt that the ideologies of the new market economies already wish to smear on professional artistic activities. The artistic endeavor suffers an accelerated campaign of contempt from populist governments, while both politicians and economists advocate review of cultural production by economic standards to determine its validity or success. Those who subscribe to such economic dictatorship seem not to understand that math equations deceive when applied to an art based on subjective human perceptions, emotions and relationships. Therefore, it is not appropriate to value culture against a crude and rough assessment of its positive or negative contributions to the functioning of the economic engine. The specific purposes and functions of art should not be evaluated by a single ideological measure of value, demonstrable and quantifiable on a graph. Culture contains human relations, as well as emotional, intellectual, spiritual and social values that are not consistent with standard economic measures; cultural results are complex and cumulative and reveal themselves best in the long term—a length that exceeds the short-sighted political vision of immediate measures and gains. That such economic determinism is contemplated and implemented on the arts bodes dark times given the profound cultural, spiritual and emotional anemia afflicting our politicians and administrators. We would not consider sane any such proposition to evaluate the rewards and value of raising children by applying an economic measure of return, with the worth and value of children depending on either an immediate or future economic value to the household. Equally, our cultural production ought not to be judged by such deterministic standards of immediate economic profit. The corollary of this economic philosophy of profit is the crass utilitarian demand that art pay for itself, as a mere product of exchange between consumer and producer.

On the one hand, while I believe a certain degree of the contempt that haunts the arts should be ascribed to the ideological nature of external pressures, on the other hand I believe that we should attach some responsibility to the art of writing's own inability to renew itself: to discover new ways to raise awareness and seduce audiences by making itself relevant to contemporary concerns. The latter question I will leave for another essay. Here, I will focus on questions posed by those questioning the value of the art of writing.

1. the home of literature

The egalitarian words of that night, at first glance innocuous and harmless – "Any of you can write and could be here in this capacity as a writer"—were perhaps flattering to the audience. They diluted certain labels that unfortunately perpetuate barriers. This immediate extension of the hand looks good. It is warm and welcoming. My house is your house. Yes ... and no. A more careful analysis reveals that such words only go over well if genuine. If we are sharing something that we actually will share equally. The reality is: after the visit, the visitor is expected to return to their own home, whether they have one or not. In this case my hospitable gesture and generous intentions are just that: an expression of intent that I quixotically plant in the air, merely symbolic or allegorical. That set of simplistic words hid a conscious or unconscious demagoguery, a bid for the audience's sympathy and allegiance to his person and image.

Indeed, in the context of this meeting of writers, it would be truer to say that many of those present partook in the passion for books and the written word of literature. But not all. A few likely experience no affection whatsoever for literature. For those that did, each person arrived from distinct geographies of interests and skills in the landscape of the written word: some as closet writers, others as readers, still others as editors, maybe a few art patrons as well as various combinations of these interests, and perhaps others yet, that weave the web of literature. This is to point out that even the politicians' presence in the audience could very well simply hold political motivations, separate from any affection for literature or the craft of writing. That likelihood does not exclude the possibility of the rare politician who holds a genuine literary interest and appreciation for their involvement and contribution to the arts. Another segment of the audience would be there not because they read or appreciate literature, but because it would be a high-profile social activity for that small community; still others might be present to support colleagues and family; or just to be seen, since the arts hold a certain prestige. Social elitism and egotism remain an allure to some during the public and restricted displays of certain artistic events. That is, many of those present came to visit the home of literature but do not reside in the house of literature.

I wonder: had this been a meeting of surgeons or carpenters, or even football players, would the audience have nodded in agreement with the statement that in fact there was no distinction between such professionals and the other citizens in the audience, and that all of us could surgically operate on cataracts, play for the country's football team or maybe even carve a mahogany desk? Yes, I know some of us enjoy kicking the ball around, and from time to time, shoulder to shoulder with a dozen sleepy friends pursuing the faster old days, we chase this world-shaped leather toy. Some of us even manage to score the occasional goal on our weekly

Saturday morning game to keep the love-handles at bay. However, in respect to surgery, while I might extract splinters and brambles from bleeding fingers, I would never venture into more complicated interventions, hence I would not dare to enter the practice of such surgical matters. I also know how to hammer a nail, almost always hit it with my swing, and I have even built my own dining table, only a bit warped. That does not mean I can produce well thought-out, solid, functional furniture, beaming with rare beauty, with any appreciable degree of consistency. My table, in fact, lives in a permanent bow of solidarity to the Tower of Pisa. In sum: I play football but I am not a footballer, I swing a hammer but I am not a carpenter, and would consider identifying myself as such to be an insult to the true professionals or artisans who dedicate and commit their lives to their activities. I am a curious dabbler and amateur in these disciplines. Those artists, proud of their merits and contributions, proud of their profession, would possibly not feel honored and appreciated if I reduced their art to a commonplace field where anyone could suddenly become a qualified and respected professional.

One of the possible interpretations contained in the statement made in this meeting is the premise that anyone who writes is a writer. Steeped in this statement is the assumption that writing is easy. What merits the status of being a writer ... is writing—the ability to handle the tools and materials of assembling words—without questioning the need to evaluate the end result. As long as I claim to juggle the letters of the alphabet, there is no need to evaluate the level of my dexterity. The accepted subtext is also saying: it is so easy to be a writer, all I need is to place a platoon of words on parade on the page and announce, "Job done." It's not possible to fail; all you need is to march ahead and fire up those sentences. Forgetting that the distance between fire and misfire is a lean one. Particularly in the mist of delusion. This premise does not include a measure of quality and accuracy. Writing, in fact, may be easier for some than for others. So where are the quality requirements, which distinguish any activity? Professionalism does not depend on the unreliable inspiration. Imagine the cabinet-maker: "Sorry, boss, the designer cabinets are not ready yet, and I do not know when they will be. Maybe in two months? Perhaps by then I hope the muse of inspiration will make a stop in my workshop. She must have lost the way in the meanwhile."

A professional masters the techniques of the craft using them how and when they want them; a professional controls his or her creative field and carries in a breast pocket the keys of access to their talent. The doors of inspiration are opened at will. The amateur shoots many darts toward the target and occasionally hits the red spot. It's luck. It happens even to the worst of us. The professional evolves in their art, and the foundations of technique are the springboard for increasingly daring jumps of spontaneity and inspiration.

Have we forgotten that the definition of a writer must fulfill the requirement to write consistently well? This measure includes any writing, from the literary to the technical and journalistic, from academic to critical writing.

I ask myself, what would move the audience to take that bait of a false promise, the claim that *anyone can write literature*? It reminds me of the old Wild West prop-up scenario in which people inserted their heads in the cut-out hole, and voilà ... anyone instantly became the most dexterous cowboy in town, complete with holster, starred chest and ten-gallon hat. With the speed of a photographic click, our lives and identities changed radically, and so did our commitments and sensibilities. To preserve this very metamorphosis, I kept such a photo to prove to my future grandchildren that for a day, I too had been a cowboy. A day, indeed. Alas, the burlesque carnival of Halloween is the trope that has conquered the arts. Today, I will disguise myself as a poet and climb the stage to live my poetic fantasy. Today, I will call myself a poet.

Has the art of writing become an easy target for those hungry to be bathed in fifteen minutes of fame? The temptation to inflate the ego remains ubiquitous, and the resulting public spectacle has become ridiculous, savagely exploited and encouraged by the commercial media which clogs air time and entertains the viewer with an embarrassing menu of shallow entertainment. That media universe feeds on the desperate souls seeking crumbs of attention at any price.

Reports of literary success, stemming from citizens catapulted from anonymity to literary stardom, proliferate in these times, even if, in most cases, they reflect a mercurial and ephemeral limelight. Success alone is an unreliable measure of competence and quality. French fries and root beer are also bestsellers in the fast food chain industry. It does not mean they are good for you or provide the nutrients you need in a meal. The present day media conglomerates yield such power that whatever they decide to push on the consumer it will be certain to succeed. You will see and hear it everywhere to exhaustion. You will dream about it. They can make people addicted to eating and craving cardboard if they wish, as long as they coat it in sugar and deep fry it.

Nowadays, I hear that everyone has a book inside them. A story dying to be told. One proliferating example is the literature of confession, disguised as fiction, which mines the memories of childhood, adolescence, and marriage, and with greater or lesser disguises, reveals its basis as an autobiographical work. Filmmakers like Kosturica sometimes use the unassuming citizen, lending a fresh and natural air to their acting on the screen. So far so good: the challenge of living my own life and portraying my own experience should not be a difficult role to play on a film set. After all, I rehearse my own life daily, from wakeup to bedtime. Now, ask that same citizen to successively dramatize Henry VIII, then Pessoa, passing through the role of Anaïs Nin or Joan of Arc, and the limitations of the actor or actress become evident. In short, this actor is condemned to act himself and no one else for the remainder of their acting careers. The same applies in literature. Day after day, year after year, it is easier to write about what I know, than to invent and write about what I do not know. It's a challenge to imagine, to research, to build worlds and different characters, patiently casting the line in hope of catching that perfect and elusive word lurking in the depths of the seas, or better yet, seeking those other words perched high on the ridges of the wind.

2. the shield of subjectivity

Literary writing is subjective. That is its strength, its spaciousness of being. Yet, to conclude that writing's subjectivity implies no need for a criteria to evaluate it, is a dangerous leap. While the boundaries of this creative territory may appear vast, such boundaries do exist. As a writer and editor I have learned that the quality of writing in a text stands out at once. Excellent writing distinguishes itself. The poor writing distinguishes itself even more readily. After reading four hundred poems submitted for consideration in each issue of our literary magazine *filling Station*, the amateur and careless work became self-evident. These works were imitative, afloat in clichés, works yet to ripen and still smelling of manure, requiring time and alchemy to compost them. Equally self-evident was the work that demonstrated a solid construction, imbued with conceptual and aesthetic qualities. From time to time, I also found the rare poem which reached the level of superb. The latter, I stress, a very rare occurrence. The ingredients which in my assessment raise a work to the sublime include: freshness, innovation, surprise, clarity, a complex plurality of meanings, emotional and intellectual acumen. These extremes at either end of the spectrum of quality being easily distinguished, the average ones remain .... well, average. In this middle range the degrees of distinction can indeed be more subjective.

I have my own literary bias in the same way that I have my culinary predispositions. "You know, I never really enjoyed the taste of coriander, do not appreciate it, but the dish does smell appetizing and is well presented. I'll pass. Bon appétit to you, anyway." I have the ability also to discern when something is unpalatable to me: it's burned or it is too uncooked for my taste. When I write something that goes amiss in the creative cooking process, I do not serve it to others; it returns to the land to feed the animals and plants, to fertilize the field of creative imagination again.

In a garden, the showy and fragrant flowers do not impress the human eye when they are dwarfed or diluted by the crowd of weeds. The masterful writer is aware that the secret is not as much in the chosen plant as in eradicating the weed, and so, on knees and hands, and slowly, very slowly, she or he weeds their garden of weak, unnecessary words. Thoroughly, by their roots, the writer extracts that which does not belong to their vision of the text. All those words in excess are ruthlessly culled, their population density minimized, the writer airing phrases and refreshing sentences and the ideas therein contained. The writer creates space for the focused words, for the gleaming flower to stand out. Sometimes I even cut down other lush flowers, sacrificing them in order to highlight the essence of those which are truly the focus of my attention. The writer understands the role of being at the service of a garden, not a slave to their self-conceit. The sloppy writer will perhaps successfully sow the same number of words, but these are overshadowed by a thicket of excesses. The reader becomes lost among the verbiage of fuzzy images; the non-distilled thoughts lack lucidity, trip over tangled redundancies. The beauty lies not in the object itself, but perhaps more fundamentally in the way beauty is framed, in that which is not shown, in all that is missing around it, that which is removed to accent the space or the silence around these few, indispensable words.

The very proposal of an evaluative criteria may seem impossibly subjective, yet its need is imperative to define and establish parameters of quality in a profession and in the work arising from it. Establishing this discerning criteria is a starting point for regenerating the art, without forgetting that it is essential not to allow these criteria to eventually underpin a dogma and to remain static in time and place.

That writer's statement communicated the presumption that writing a novel, a play, a coherent manuscript of poetry, requires no technical knowledge and mastery of this art. Even if invisible to the untrained eye, there are technical aspects in the telling of a story that contribute to the narrative functioning or not. Works of word masters possess a skill and an effortless flow that is easily mistaken for ease of implementation. As if drawn with a natural effortlessness that we all believe is a universal experience within everyone's reach. The combination of technical, narrative, linguistic, imagistic, and syntactical tools, along with inspiration, create a whole not only intelligible and rational, but also of rare beauty. From this synergistic preparation the magic of art is born. The whole surpasses the mere accumulation of its parts.

Aesthetic evolution contains a certain temporal-historical relativism. If a particular century appreciates the sonnet, then another appreciates free verse. On the other hand, we also encounter works of greater resistance to the erosion of time and to the volatility of fashion, as shown by the epic of Gilgamesh, The Odyssey, The Lusiads, the Koran, the Bible, the Bhagavad-Gita, among others. The immortal mix of ingredients demonstrates vast appeal and longevity. These works illustrate a quasi-universal appeal that connects with the different abilities of each listener. Depending on the reader's experience and ability, they will find their unique and personal point of entry into the work and will experience something unique as well as something widely shared in this engagement. In contrast, a would-be writer showing disdain for necessary fluency in the field of basic writing techniques draws a naive vision of the craft, believing that anyone can fake their way and miraculously create something of artistic merit. Immaculate conception does not exist in art, as Walter Kuhn kindly reminded us.

Some individuals do consciously or unconsciously exercise a sense of innate mastery of these story-telling techniques, whether acquired by observation, modeling or intuition, or perhaps even by genetic inheritance. (In unravelling the genetic coil, we may one day, discover that the weekly broccoli in the family diet pattern, also aided in building a healthy density to the bone structure of a sentence.)

Who has not encountered the same anecdote or story told by different people and with different results? The effective and ineffective storyteller are distinguished by how the audience is captivated or not. In one case the audience disappears, and if it cannot disappear, it yawns, jitters or falls asleep in the chair. In the opposite experience, listeners are mesmerized by the word and become rooted to their seat. We all can tell a story. We are not all equal as storytellers.

If most of what is published in the literary world is of inferior quality, the magnetic force of art is weakened in its ability to evolve and renovate in order to attract new enthusiasts. If only one in ten times that I nibble on a persimmon, the fruit leaves me sufficiently excited to bow before its marvel of full-flavoured sweetness, then the other nine times it will end up revealing its sour or astringent taste. As a consequence, very soon, I will switch to eating plums. I know that those growers have scruples and the chances of finding a sour note upon my palate are remote. Plums will soon become my trusted fruit of choice. All persimmon growers will lose in the absence of rigor and criteria of quality in their industry. Even the persimmon creators with scruples striving to only offer and harvest the mature and robust fruit will eventually lose, betrayed by unscrupulous colleagues lending a bad name to the profession. Hence, in the name of self-preservation these persimmon growers need to establish minimum parameters to separate the sweet from the bitter and to preserve the reputation of the profession.

An artistic profession requires the artist to create works of merit with a high degree of consistency. The higher the bar, the more respect and admiration the art will receive. The creation of self-imposed criteria and strict requirements of quality, followed by the reinforcement of such criteria by publishers, critics, editors, the reading public, literary organizations and our own fellow writers, contributes to an effective accumulation of filters in order to provide final work with high quality. In my experience, if it is already challenging to be an evaluator of the work of others, and harder still to be an unsuspected assessor of one's own work. An external perspective counterbalances our creative strabismus because we are too close to the subject: writing is an extension of ourselves. I would emphasize that the issue of identification of levels of professionalism in the writing arts is not merely a matter of institutionally validated expertise or attained financial success in the pursuit of such activity. Already, too many professionals in varied areas of the labour market demonstrate their competence by means of a certificate attesting to their expertise. Conversely, a pedestrian history of punching the daily clock does not in itself make you competent at what you do.

3. with or without a magnifying glass

To emphasize the elements and instruments involved in judging the value of a work of art, let us consider two extremes: the casual reader and the professional critic. Both are appreciators of culture, although their point of contact with the work differs.

By and large, the casual reader is distanced from the core and the mechanical aspects of the art. They connect with the artistic experience in a distanced and informal manner, purely aesthetic and emotional. This in itself provides immense value since it evaluates the versatility of the work, whether the work contains ingredients that captivate a wide range of interests regardless of the specific skills of the particular art receptor. The casual reader approaches the work without gloves, tweezers and magnifying glass; and also without the guardedness of inherent prejudices and ideologies existent in the bickering art world. In general, this reader opts for an emotional encounter with the word, foregoing the cerebral, dissecting and analytical approaches. He or she does not have the bias of a technical lens that filters and predetermines the approach to the work, that accentuates certain vices and distortions inherent in its proximity to the profession. If the casual reader does not find immediate resonance with the work, they will not walk on eggshells. They will dump it without ceremony or hesitation, burying it in the catacombs of the mind. The work has not established a contact point for this reader; or the reader did not want to expend the energy and time required to find their meeting point. Perhaps they were not familiar with the language of the discipline and were not equipped with its entry code. The casual reader tends to feel captivated by a work within their preferred aesthetic language and accessible to their personal framework of values, reflecting their experience and interests. In all likelihood, most will not want to be forced to stretch their intellectual or aesthetic territory of comfort; they will lean toward the usual diet of approachable and digestible works. This reader will gravitate to that which distracts, a body of work somewhat predictable in its diet of happy endings. They are not a fan of jolts to the foundation that sustains their reality; they do not seek an artistic experience that will lead to further exploring the complexity and conflicts that permeate their world. They prefer to evade that reality, prefer an experience that will reaffirm the values and perceptions already accepted and incorporated into their way of being, seeing and experiencing the world. An experience that will ensure, with a pat on the back, all is well in her or his cosmos, as well as in the vast universe. The casual reader does not enjoy seeing the architecture of their building and possessions, or the decor of their values, challenged, least of all demolished.

Knowledgeable of the form and committed to the specific discipline, the competent professional critic, or even any refined reader with a critical view, tends to be more sophisticated in his or her attitude and relationship with the art of writing. Experience, accumulated through years of contact with the art, has coached their keenness of perception. A trained eye is quick to identify what it has practiced identifying within its expected scope. Yet, it can also grow addictive, indolent along repetitive pathways of travel, and become unresponsive to change, uninterested in integrating aspects of renewal it may encounter.

On the positive side, the critic is familiar with the complexity of the access codes to the discipline. Already understands, and perhaps is even fluent, in their dialect. Practice and experience allow more subtle and complex comparisons and distinctions, which extend to the micro-cosmos of a work and reveal its inherent complexity. In my eyes, the most admirable expert tends to reject the commonplace, recognizes the work's jurisdiction and clamors before the innovative creation that reinvents and challenges the norms of reading, that redefines the discipline and propels it to evolve.

All that is created, including artistic creation, does not arise from a vacuum. Both creation and appreciation of art do not occur in isolation. Both the writer and the reader absorb the art in comparison to the existing body of that art, the entire body of creation that precedes a new work and beside which it will be compared. The evaluation is done in this comparative context whether the judge wants to be aware of this reality or not. The art is thus absorbed in a discriminated way already. The judging of a work and the emotional experience of a work are not elements that converge automatically in relation to the assessment of this experience or art. I may feel affection for a work simply because the work is the effort of a person dear of even acquainted with me. Both the work and author being evaluated emotionally converge to the territory of my personal proximity; I cannot remove the emotional context of my acquaintance with the author; and as I am privy to the circumstances surrounding the preparation of the work, the intimacy of meanings contained in the work, those ingredients are set against the chronology of the author's life. What I feel during my evaluation is real and personal, not an unbiased assessment of the work of art in itself. The work does not exist as an object external to the individual concerned, outside of their personhood. My evaluation would therefore be warped or even incomprehensible to readers lacking access to these details, intimacies and emotions that influence my reading of the work. Logically, readers would feel cheated by my expert reading, when faced with the missing colors in the pages I had so exalted.

The necessary proximity to the literary communities, which critics observe and evaluate, is in itself already a reality that requires the critic to exercise due awareness and self-examination for unfair bias. However, a new development has upped the ante of literary criticism to a new problematic realm. An independent, impartial eye is an increasingly difficult challenge to achieve, since contemporary literary critics are now also literary creators and have become enmeshed in complex social webs of affection within the discipline, enmeshed in its envies and power struggles, its claims for attention and competitive trophy hunting, a never-ending plot of intrigues. Hence, the need to rescue the role of the independent critical eye, removed from these emotional currents of subjectivity and personal interests; an all important quest for the integrity of literature and its evaluation. Or in the very least, every review and reviewer should include in footnote a range of compulsory caveats informing the readers about the level of proximity to the work and writer. From an "I have slept with the author," to "I have only slept with the book" range of disclosure.

If in film we have managed to retain the role of the professional critic without the need for them to be filmmakers, why are we not capable of supporting professional literary critics and reviewers?

Ultimately, the critical evaluation of a creative work is not more than a comment on the meeting or the un-meeting between the sender and receiver of such art. The result of this dance: in sync or not in sync? Expectations fulfilled or frustrated? And by extension, this judgment is perhaps a mutual comment on the universe inhabited by the receiver and the transmitter. A direct comment, a criticism, a praise, reveal not only the evaluation criteria of the receiver, but an equal measuring bar for evaluating those very demands of the receiver/critic. How high have they set their measuring bar? This is a two-way street. A comment on the work indirectly reveals the inner architecture of the critic. Evaluations may reverberate far and wide around the world, yet they should never be taken as the one and only definitive judgement of the work. The work itself is immutable, the words will never slip off the page. The approach to the reading, the brightness or not of the mind which drinks the work, the hummed values in the broadcasting and receiving of language, the cultural buzz in the background, these are a few of the ever-changing elements encountering the book and its words across time, culture and space. The perception and commentary on a work present a vast field of possibilities and variations, a consequence of that approaching angle, that orbit, that meeting or un-meeting between the work and its reader.

4. art and democracy

Art originates from all social classes. In proposing criteria to measure standards of quality, I may be accused of proposing nothing more than a subjective statement of class, perpetuating a group of conventions dominant in the arts; charged that I am blind to the arrogance and discrimination inherent in these parameters. Is, then, rigor or upholding degrees of rigor an attribute of a certain class only?

The participation of a person in the artistic world most often has implicated a premise of class consciousness and privilege. Writing always requires an apprenticeship period that entails access to the wealth of open time or the access to financial resources that meet survival needs while no income is being generated, often for long periods of time, if not a lifetime. The artist believes he or she has something to say or to show and that the world, or certain worlds, will listen. Usually the higher classes breathe this self-confidence in their daily existence. Raised in this cradle of entitlement and belief, they will embrace art with determination carrying their automatic assumption of the right to broadcast and the assurance they will be paid attention to. The aura of importance with which the privileged class sees itself, together with the corresponding attention given to them by the other classes wanting to emulate them, imbues the upper class with an advantageous point of departure.

Nonetheless, democracy has at last, and none too soon, reached the shores of the arts. Although the distinction between high and popular culture has not been thoroughly dissipated, we are moving toward a gradual and sustained process of deconstruction of the old walls of exclusivity. In this century, I don't need to be nobility to set fingers to a piano. The possibility of appreciation and participation in all artistic domains is now accessible to an ever-increasing number of citizens. The door to dreaming is now open. Unlike nocturnal dreams, however, where lounging in our beds, we picture that we are climbing Mt. Everest without spilling a drop of sweat on the pillow, the everyday dreams of wakefulness demand a cascade of sweat. Democracy requires work, responsibility and involvement by the citizen, and it rewards those who venture to offer the streaming salt of sacrifice.

The need for self-expression and communication is universal. Many people are capable of writing, and many show potential or even evidence of having something to add to the literary sensibility. Many, but not all. Many could, but many will not. They will not, because the commitment required to be a writer requires sacrifices, perseverance and long-term dedication to a path that may or may not arrive at loving and being loved by the public. No assurances here.

True notoriety requires a posture of risk and adventure toward the unknown. The map is being drawn while travelling the course of this journey. Few individuals have the temperament to dwell outside the unmapped and the normative boundaries. This is true in any sphere of human experience. For those who venture to distinguish themselves from the rest of humanity in their various fields, society reserves a degree of notoriety which helps postpone the perpetual anonymity that mortality will bring. For even fewer, those standing in the banished ranks we call radicals, it will bring the additional bonus of exile, crucifixion and martyrdom for having dared to step outside normative behaviour and/or speak up against the almighty powers. These artists are portrayed as monsters, vermin, and carriers of the infectious malady threatening to unsettle the quiet mundanity of the herd.

I insist on the need to distinguish the competence that evolves from a gaze of consistent contemplation, a gaze committed to language and writing; articulating a visionary imagination, both inventive and discerning. At this level of intensity and investment of time and energy, something emerges that is distinguished from a mere sideways or erratic glance toward the discipline. Indeed, that is why these artistic pursuits used to be called *disciplines*. Those committed to such contemplation, despite feeling the pleasure and pain of everyday life, develop attributes and achieve unmatched experiences to which the public has access through the appreciation of such artistic production.

The relative performance of the amateur or of the professional athlete in the sports world clearly sets the two apart. Therefore we identify those differences by using a word, a lexicon that distinguishes and honors the different realities and results. Both amateur and professional universes are fundamental in strengthening our social fabric. The hour of distinguishing the efforts of amateurs and professionals in the written arts and recognizing and compensating them accordingly is overdue.

It is not my intention to silence those who want to dip a foot in the arts. The pleasure that any amateur activity brings to participants and to the community is a spiritual, social and emotional asset that must be welcomed and encouraged in any society. Does this mean we throw open every stage floor for all to democratically empty the fireworks of their thoughts upon the world? Should we not exercise discernment and establish guidelines, demand a proven record to determine the competence of those wanting to step on a pulpit? In the same way, I do not choose to live with a person with a motor-mouth, constantly spewing everything that travels through their mind, without discernment, without respect for the sacredness of silence. Silence should be only interrupted with great humility and only when we have something relevant to contribute to the conversation. The silence surrounding words highlights their importance, assures us that the word was weighed, polished, contemplated, and deserves the light of day. Words without such reins are excessively dumped in the sea of everyday life, such as one purges interior contaminants—dumped far away from us into an atmosphere that we unconsciously pollute and which we all share. Such words exorcise our private dementias but ironically saturate the art until it risks drowning in a bog of mushy cacophony. Not every personal diary must be published and made public. Please, please.

I would emphasize that these distinctions between quality and mediocrity, between amateurism and professionalism, are not intended as arguments to defend the scholarly and erudite against the popular, and thus perpetuate hierarchies within the written arts, a reflection or mere extension of the existing social hierarchies. Despite arguments and bickering between popular and scholarly forms of art, in regard to their cataloging and classification, elevation or contempt, central or peripheral values, labels as major or minor depending on how they relate to class and hierarchies of subjugation, none of these issues belongs to the scope of this discussion, and would require a more specific analysis. This popular versus scholarly duality, infused with a sense of class distinction, must always be questioned as well as its inherent exclusivity. Still I propose and insist on this need for quality standards in literary production and evaluation, despite its degree of subjectivity and arbitrariness. Such standards will always reflect an intrinsic and defining criteria which reflects the sensitivity and the culture of a self-identified group. I believe that beyond that perpetual slippery territory of definitions, a pure intention exists in an effort to create a demand for standards of excellence. Just as I seek a quality fabric in a garment, I seek the best quality ingredients in the making of a culinary dish; ingredients which reflect the highest commitment in its creation, and performance to deliver superior satisfaction.

The reader might argue that my reasoning extols an old song that glorifies and defends class divisions which for centuries have been preventing popular participation and are overdue to be demolished. Allow me to refine the argument. The distinction is subtle, yet important. Erecting walls to separate individuals for reasons external to their performance, value and ability, solely to preserve territories of privilege, stems from a different intention than that of indentifying distinct abilities of performance. In the latter case, the distinction welcomes anyone who meets the criteria and can fulfill their function within these criteria—whosoever demonstrates competence to belong to this group. Consider the swimming pool where I occasionally go to float my spare tire, and being a slow-motion swimmer, a swimmer of frequent stops to verify whether the clock actually is still moving, I never occupy the lane of the dolphin-like swimmers, those who do not swim but skim the water. My place is in the turtle lane in order not to clog up the traffic flow and the enjoyment of the pool by all. If I wanted to dedicate myself to swimming, that lane would be open to me as long as my performance matched the parameters for speed and endurance expected there. Of course I would never dare to enter a swim meet with the pros, unless I had been hired as an underwater clown.

5. goals and targets

When one recites, *we are all equal and we can all achieve the same goals*, such ideology strums the chords of solidarity and camaraderie. Yet, we are not all born equal in all respects; at best we are born with innate similarities as humans. Our goals are not necessarily confluent since our interests are not identical. What is most at issue here is the reality that our capabilities and skills differ.

After we enter a circle of competence, in which a fine bricklayer is a fine bricklayer, a fine writer is a fine writer, a fine tailor is a fine tailor, there is yet an additional dimension that distinguishes exceptional talent. There are bricklayers and then there are bricklayers, there are writers and then there are writers, and deep in the heart of hearts we know where we dwell and where we belong in this wider context. It is not flattering to pretend to be more than what we are, nor to pretend we are less than what we are. In both cases we invite disrespect for our lack of authenticity; we demonstrate ignorance of who we are, our values and our role as weavers of intricate patterns that enhance the complexity of our community fabric.

To encourage all citizens to explore their creative abilities, their hidden or neglected potential, is a fundamental process of human development. It stimulates self-awareness, mutual understanding and personal, social, cultural and civic participation in our communities. In addition, we will also cultivate art aficionados, sophisticated and demanding connoisseurs, who certainly will challenge art and artists to further their creative, critical and interventionist visions. Sophisticated aficionados and citizens will not easily allow the wool to be pulled over their eyes.

Perhaps one day every one of us will be capable of excelling and achieving notoriety in different areas of artistic, technologic, and economic expression, a member of a truly evolved species. True multifaceted beings, inspired by the Renaissance vision and the multifaceted genius capabilities of a Leonardo Da Vinci. Until we meet that future, I will give my house nails a hammering, will kick the football about and participate in numerous activities that express my creativity, while never forgetting that another dimension exists where the true professionals engage body and soul in their respective fields and demonstrate a gift for which my eyes widen, my mouth falls ajar and I make a long bow of appreciation and recognition. I emphasize that art can be a book, a pair of shoes, an opera, a magnificent free-kick goal, a sublime and original dessert custard. If these artists do not suffer from inflated egos, they will immediately recognize that this bow is not of subservience, rather a genuine salute to the human spirit that briefly approached the greatness and divine image of their creator, and shared their unique work with us.

Vale de Cambra / 2004

CANADA TREADS UPON OUR BOOKS

A new phenomenon of combative books adorned with spikes rather than spines, armours rather than covers, vying for centre stage and the gold medal of attention at the annual CBC *Canada Reads* marketing blitz, has become the prominent public spectacle of our Canadian literary scene.

The essential design of this radio show—yes show, not program—borrows the militaristic "shock and awe" tactic to reveal the one and only winner by applying the psychological counterpart of the gory attrition of Roman gladiators or ice hockey goons to drum up the attention of listeners. The authors themselves are not required to step onto this cerebral bloodthirsty rink to be pitted against each other, as one would expect of a sweaty-browed hockey league soldier where the broken nose and missing teeth are worn with the pride of a warrior flaunting his survival wounds to the audience.

Instead, *Canada Reads* relies on a group of surrogate book lawyers, AKA book defenders, themselves national media icons, who wield the brick-shaped book of their fancy, and articulate or not with their words—in this show, verbal dexterity and intellectual acuity are not necessary skills to evaluate books—as they proceed to whack their book impressions over each other's heads and presumed wits, use tactical voting manoeuvres against perceived strong contenders while employing strategies of elimination borrowed from another grandparent show of greater TV fame, Survivor. This literary cannibalistic feast continues until one defending book lawyer emerges from the populist literary battle field, standing alone beneath the shower of applause.

The poster face for this show, Jian Gomeshi, I regard as a thoughtful human being who reveals the candour of his spirit and the sensibility of his heart in engaging interviews with cultural personalities. Without question, he is a man of notable depth, overflowing with energy and generosity for the promotion of cultured disciplines. We are fortunate to have him in this country. Nevertheless, I wonder whether this model of bringing culture to the nation in a gut-punching format deemed appealing to the masses, truly benefits the cultural workers, in our case, the writers. I assume Jian Gomeshi believes in what he does. Otherwise this is a misstep he knows not how to disentangle himself from, and he is not telling us so. I do sense his moments of discomfort after a particular ugly punch has flown through the airwaves, leaving in many a home a taste of acrid blood on the tongue, while Jian hurries into the rink—a late-arriving referee seeking a diplomatic intervention to remedy the situation. Can he speak his truth on air?

Since I consider Jian an intelligent, captivating pop culture worker and a man yielding significant influence over the cultural shape of this country, I am disappointed that he appears unable to think outside this very large and country-wide populist radio-box catering to low-common denominator emotions aimed at audience harvesting. On the other hand, perhaps that is the reason such personalities become the media giants they become: they are frantically juggling all the sugar-balls in the air, luring audiences in order to stay in the limelight themselves. Media personalities do not seem to find time to stop and contemplate the more far-reaching tendrils of their actions. No pause, no space appears in which to ponder the next step, to re-evaluate the integrity of the present path. Is he unwilling or rather incapable of carving alternative paths on this literary landscape and generate a more intelligent conversation about books? Is he a good-natured driver on a track-bound train no longer knowing how to pull the frays?

The argument that this is the culture we inhabit and therefore writers must corroborate, so as to receive a slice of the attention pie, perpetuates the tradition of oppressive systems that portray themselves as the only alternative and sole viable reality. Once such imprint of understanding burrows in the mind of a citizen, the rest becomes a swift slide-down-the-tube to literary wasteland.

In this Canada, I have grown to expect, though not accept, the proliferating spectacles of aggressive fusion—roller-skate derbies with Greco-Roman wrestling in the mix, World Wrestling with staged clichéd drama, ice hockey and its pugilistic displays. A combative posture and elimination of the other are essential postulates in the popular culture as sought and promoted by the centralized media interests. The horror of witnessing this genre of promotion landing at the feet of books and literature has left me as dizzy as any of those wrestlers and hockey players after a punch to the jaw, and I wonder whether one can think properly with such an aggressive impact freezing one's brain. We should ask Sidney Cosby, Steve Moore and all others in the long list of victims, how they feel and why they keep returning for more servings of the same. Why do audiences return for more since there is no spectacle without spectators?

Audiences and players return for servings of more high drama and gore, the same way they return for more sugar, fat and salt in their fast foods. They are addictive ingredients. One becomes dependent on these behavioral or chemical patterning pathways after being raised amid such diets, visual or otherwise. After a time its presence even becomes comforting and necessary once it is integrated into one's identity. That is why corporations push themselves into baby cradles, schools and children's sports in order to stamp their corporate, consumer imprint very early and become incorporated in the human DNA behaviour of a culture. This makes it extremely difficult for the individual to unplug or see through the tainted air they already breathe.

Of all disciplines, and in the awakening times we live, I would have expected the literary written word to seek deeper roots in its transformative vein and not succumb to its *Entertainment Ville* escapist genetics which *Canada Reads* offers. If I am to have a transformative impact in the world as a cultural worker it is my vocation to re-imagine the landscape that surrounds us, to engage our collective imagination in redesigning the civic processes of interaction in order to achieve more fulfilling and wholesome experiences of community. My literature is not made in the service of preserving status quo or legitimatizing oppression and violence, mindless escapism and resignation. I do not expect to walk down the road of the NHL temples where human beings are pitted against each other and encounter a peaceful evening of non-sectarian community-building, an evening without the neurotic highs and lows of winning and losing over which I as an individual have no control; unless, and until, I and you, change the dominant cultural paradigm and refocus our priorities, dispense our limited time and energy to other edifying projects than the cold soul-on-ice. Nothing will change until we refuse to participate in events that perpetuate undercurrents of exploitative and aggressive values. The medium is the message, regardless of the seasonal change of flavours in the content.

Jian has proven to carry a sufficient number of brain cells in his thinking kit to be capable of re-imagining a program which honours the lives of books and the magic of reading, a place where the aim is collaborative, respectful, and the ambience is nourishing, not cutting. Then, the electricity in the air grows not from anxiety nor fear, not from survival nor defeat, rather from beauty, excellence and empathy. The word is cherished both as an end and a medium. So why hasn't Jian re-imagined a different conversation over this cultural medium, one equally captivating, engaging intelligent people who function as creatively as the objects before them? It could be a quest for a treasure where we decipher codes and unearth hidden labyrinths until we arrive at the last page to enjoy the fruits of the view and savour the accomplishment of all arriving with a deeper understanding of the journey. It could become an exploration of books which, over time, have brought the world to shift its mind, its understanding of itself and its place in it, as accomplished by books such as: *On the Origin of Species, The King James Bible, Don Quixote, One Thousand and One Nights, War and Peace, The Silent Spring, 1984, Walden,* and Shakespeare's plays. It could also become a celebration, including a new or deeper learning, about a book that transformed the life path of a person, their intimate story and relationship to that book. Or how yet another book brought a couple together by their mutual esteem for words, the moment they fell in love with each other as they shared aloud, and by the streetlight, the poetry of e.e. cummings. It could also be the story of a reader who returned to the same book one hundred times, and an account of the different and new things he or she found in each reading. In this process of attentive listening to the intimate stories of other people with their books, we might learn more deeply about a certain book and its intricacies and nuances. In the same vein, we can, of course, also explore the books that brought intolerance, death and destruction to humanity and to certain individuals.

In the presence of passion, excellence and beauty in books, resorting to mudslinging in a program about literature is unnecessary since the attention of the audience is naturally engaged in the discovery. Think of Harold Bloom, Joseph Campbell, Wade Davis or Alberto Manguel as passionate storytellers, spellbinders of the word. I believe in such a world and invest my energy and effort in supporting related initiatives, which is the reason to write these words.

Allow me to imagine a cultural experience with a level playing field and no podium or pyramid—rather a wide circle that includes many, where quality and differences are cherished and we join to celebrate the art of writing and reading. It is no longer the menace of the goon behind the work, shoving it down your throat that proves what is worthwhile. The day we cherish skill over force, we in the Wild West might at last, as Gandhi once postulated, enter the gates we call civilization.

I may hold limited control over the fate of my books and to which cultural tribunals they are submitted in order to be weighed and lashed to measure for their strength; yet from my core principles and of my free will, I cannot envision allowing my works sacrificed in this spectacle-drama of the modern literary gladiator rink of *Canada Reads*.

Would I send the birthing effort of my heart: book or child, into a setting where the only possibility of having her or his skills recognized, the beauty of its individuality, the achievements and particular gifts of their existence celebrated, would rest in a weeklong knockout-trial system of schoolyard violence, plotting strategies to bring all others down, amid the irrational cheerleading of parents on the sidelines inciting a win at any cost? Will this be a valid measure of the worthiness of a human being or of a book, of acknowledging their contribution to our society? I think not.

I name this and all other forms of aggression as a long-promoted system of acquiescence and social normalization embedded in Hollywood flicks and countless other pop culture servings where the trumpets rise at the end of the story to elevate the last man standing—yes, usually a man— the hero, saviour, the superman. The community, the society is rarely depicted as the hero, the collective effort seldom shown as the sustaining cradle that permits the ephemeral flashes of the individual. Who is left to recount the story of the defeated in the games of gore? Perhaps the invisibility of the defeated and their stories may be the reason why we are still entangled in the dark shadows of the atrocities that gave birth to the nations of this continent, from slaughter and slavery to indigenous residential schools, and why we continue addicted to violence and its promotion—always disguised as reality, while its fabrication remains hidden— requiring our acceptance or participation to endure. Violence is familiar, and we have tasted it from the first slap on the buttocks. Violence has been normalized, socialized and idolized ... and has dulled us. Our nerve endings have been pounded to numbness.

In its many manifestations, from the physical to the verbal, violence is validated, through interaction and play, civic and institutional modeling. I only need to listen to the Canadian Parliament in action for a crude example. Let me not become sidetracked here. Imagine *Canada Reads* does become my week-long dream of fame. At the end, were my own book to survive the knockout rounds to arrive at such dizzying heights of victorious grandeur and crowned the bully of the schoolyard *Canada Reads* promo show, then I might believe myself or my book child so very special. After all, a few other thousand or million followers appear to corroborate the prize. However, with the frenetic spin of fads and fashions, the audience moves their attention to the next sacrificial lamb or gladiator about to step into the rink for the next yearly round of grind and gore. The moment you are crowned you have begun the descent to forgotten, and the cycle again begins.

After the height of the trumpets, one must not neglect to report finding those stale heroes of yesterday in late-night bars folded over the stupor of an empty bottle, staring at the glimmering glass, seeking a brief reflection of past heights, attempting to recover the feel-good needle in the haystack of fickle fate. The inevitable fall from such peaks has shattered their fragile egos which are the reason they sought such heights in the first place.

I have never enjoyed the attribution of literary prizes, even though with my first time in print I have been guilty of participating in the competitive ritual of prizes, swallowing the hook with the smooth line, having recognized such limelight necessary to my professional economic survival. When during a prize finalist's reading, already privately having been informed I had received the prize, I suggested in public we should simply share the prize. No winner. Or better yet: All Winners. Everyone laughed, possibly interpreting my words as a joke born out of the anxiety of not knowing who the winner would be.

Prizes have become the live or die book marketing game in town. The stakes have grown that much higher, the competition steeper, the desperation descending that much deeper. In the context of this evolution of marketing strategies for writers, each vying for distinction, sparing no punches in their salvo for attention, I hope to have woken up, recognizing now the crudeness of being fed to the entertainment machine does compromise my integrity. Were the less distasteful and traditional marketing prizes such as the Booker, GG's, Giller brands to arrive knocking at my door, what would I say, and more important, what would I do? To what extent would I participate in these established rituals? I will have to measure the muck of my participation with the opportunity to speak in and from the belly of the beast. I could use that podium to make a statement and propose a more cooperative, inclusive approach, voice my desire for alternative models of recognizing value, effort, contribution, without winners and losers. Without elimination or loser lists. Perhaps I could even donate the prize to the Writer's Union for collective benefit of all writers by instituting a different recognition model of artistic life achievement, individual book realization as elected by peers, critics and readers. What path will I choose if my child needs a new pair of shoes, and I would hope to continue on a writing path? A decade later, and in a deeper vulnerable professional situation, any decision I will make regarding prize acceptances will implicate my entire family. The luxury of saying no to prize money will carry consequences for my young children's diet. It is rarely an easy choice, even less for the atypical literary writers in this country who do not have the pay cheque of academia or school boards to fall back on.

I have no doubt that *Canada Reads* will continue its inexorable march of success, building larger audiences alongside the World Wrestling and Hockey Night in Canada audiences, all vying to attract larger numbers of consumers to run their money machine, feeding on the sacrificial lamb and pushing the edges of the aggressive and the permissible. This, until the day it grossly oversteps the line with a murder on ice or a book pitch concussion, and perhaps only then prompting a pause of the scheme by the outraged. When that time arrives, another adrenaline addiction will settle in the veins of listeners, and either the roller-derby practice of literary merit becomes institutionalized or it will wither away into another dark footnote of history.

Until then, other literary cultural workers such as Sartre, Leonard Cohen, Arundhati Roy, Roald Dahl, Graham Greene, Doris Lessing, CS Lewis and Adrienne Rich, among many, many others, will continue to be discerning and decline certain awards and honors, unwilling to compromise their conscience and values despite the bait. Those and others will avoid the growing literary circus traps and continue to speak up in an attempt to create alternative models of visibility and respect for their words and ideas, proposing alternative visions on behalf of the present and the future so I, you and our children will have a true choice between a range of roads that will deliver us to distinct destinations and experiences of being—being ourselves and being in community. Then, we will be prepared to engage in our civic and cultural communities without growing up believing ice hockey is the only relevant sport in town or Canada Reads is the best way to discover amazing books.

Some defend this high-profile forum for the book as a better-than-nothing equation, as though in this competitive field of proliferating cultural objects vying for the time and attention of consumers, one should be thankful for any manner of attention books may elicit from the media. Is attention worthy at any price?

There is a word much in disuse today called *integrity*. From ministerial to corporate seats, from the street beat of our cities to our dysfunctional families, integrity, we hear, is as endangered as our polar bear and the melting principles of mutual care. In books and in the rest of our lives, the malaise of modernity reveals an increasing gap between our values and our actions, individuality and community. Each one of us must evaluate the alignment of our actions to our values, the care of one and the care of all.

Will I continue to prefer invisibility under the global literary radar over accepting a circus clown role? Indeed, I prefer to go thirsty than drink the poison water, despite the dramatic attention it elicits in the manner of a Julius Caesar re-telling of our despairing soul. I prefer to account for the long-term effects of actions, projects, relationships than taste the ephemeral high. I prefer to die sane and globally anonymous, yet whole, than to live fragmented by bipolar madness of high and lows, shock and awe.

Meanwhile, I assure you that you will not see me bless my book in that gory rink of *Canada Reads* or will I ever encourage my child to step into a pugilistic arena on ice skates. Yes, I am Canadian. My values are Canadian—of the other Canada, the larger Canada, a Canada that does not congregate around modern arenas of aggression, a Canada that may appear silent or perhaps even inexistent since our gatherings do not help to sell you or me more overpriced beer, deodorant or perfume which we don't need anyway; our gatherings without spectacle do not interest those with the muscle to throw their messages with a flick of a switch to every corner of country or planet; and therefore our gatherings go undiscovered.

Our gatherings are conversations that nourish a Canada whose citizens listen to each other, respect differences and speak intelligently in order to open more space for even more voices to join, be heard and celebrated. Not the slight we accept now, elimination by elimination; "the less" sold as more, packaged in oversized cereal boxes on supermarket shelves, shouting loud colours and promises, only half-filled yet sweetened to addictive excess. These boxes are built to deceive; it is the nature of their game. Of their game, I will not partake.

Victoria / 2011

THE STORY

1. *reincarnations*

The cyclical debate over the relevance of literature in its varied forms is revived at times when new technologies and innovative turns appear on the cultural road. It is important to distinguish between the essence of narrative and its myriad forms of expression or vehicles of delivery. Be it a Greek tragedy or an Austen novel, ghazal or villanelle, dance, visual art, computer game or song, wrapped in Super8 or iPhone, stone tablet or digital tablet, paperback or eBook, storytelling is and always will remain part of our human essence. The medium or the form in which language and narrative find their vehicle of expression will change; sonnet or computer game will encounter their apogee and demise, and while some forms will reincarnate, many others await invention. Nevertheless, stories will remain essential to our engagement with the world and each other as a vehicle of communication. It will continue allowing us to express and share our values, ideas, dreams, visions, tears, concerns, complaints and jubilations.

More importantly, questions about the future of writing lie not in the equation of technology, its advances and their varied instruments, but rather in the evolution of the storyteller. I am more concerned about the integrity of the storyteller and the formidable human qualities that role entails: resilience, maturity and fearlessness, insight and genius. I am most concerned that the storyteller who embraces the role of being the midwife of change, voice of the voiceless, speaker of inconvenient truths, is most endangered among the proliferation of writers who have opted for the role of entertainer, perpetuator of status quo, collector of privileges while focused on ego aggrandizement. Equipped with integrity and fearlessness, a storyteller inspires us to endure times of oppression and dissent, to stand one's ground and speak the forbidden, say the unsayable. This is the integrity expected from oracles, whistleblowers, witnesses and seers speaking the forbidden while the arrows rain down and the chains clink on. The dangerous times have returned, and perhaps they had never left us. Are there enough courageous storytellers alive to break the growing silences? Are there sufficient numbers of wordsmiths among us committed to speaking their truth rather than living preoccupied with ego polishing and climbing the ladder of professional accolades?

2. *resuscitation*

Word and story can function as an emergency resuscitation for our numbed selves, quagmired in hopelessness and exhaustion, buried in overworking conditions. This rubbing of words generates sparks to illuminate the atrophied mind after a diet of cultural inanity and stale laugh tracks. A fresh story may articulate a need so utterly fundamental to human longing, so deeply repressed and silent that it will resurrect the flame of desire for a different living experience. This fundamental capacity of awakening the human spirit and resurrecting the citizen by naming, remembering, connecting and informing, giving voice to that which was silenced and lies moribund, has always been the spark feared by those wishing the world asleep.

Many have believed that narrative, or any other cultural discipline, was only politically relevant insomuch as it was capable of catalyzing people, a critical mass of the masses, in order to burst the chains that bound them both to the system and to behavioural patterns of oppression.

The irony has been that often the oppressed, hungry, addicted, down-and-out are illiterate, or only functionally literate, and do not have the means or interest to access intellectual cultural tools that supposedly might save them from the bottom of the world. Their hierarchy of needs is more basic and pressing: bread and a bed.

A storymaker and teller myself, I have grown so accustomed to the company of my own head and imaginary worlds that I have developed, at best, my own language tics, or at worse, an insular language understood only by the membership of this trade. Imagine twins in their solipsistic universe of private signals which no one else can access. As for the social or political impact of those of us labouring in these secluded laboratories of language and mind, it becomes a deranged illusion to dream I may draw the interest of others, let alone inspire them to action or change, or for those more inclined to ego-idolatry, to admire an artist's already self-perceived brilliance as a writer.

Many artists, myself included, spring from a literate class of privilege or semi-privilege, with access to education and the resources or leisure to invent stories, and the self-confidence to believe such narratives could be of interest to others and perhaps make a difference in their lives. This mindset stems from a political model which supposes the citizen will be listened to and hold influence over decision-makers. When one grows up not being listened to and not taken seriously, one believes what one says is worthless, to have zero impact in the world. The maestros of power have been at this cat-and-mouse game from the beginning of time and are no fools. Let us not forget that the first professional resident artists began their lives as entertainers to the elites in the palatial courts, and their work had to please the rulers; otherwise their head might roll or, if lucky, they might only receive the boot and lose their daily bowl. Entertaining was the key word: make people laugh, not think.

More recently the *patrons* have engineered forums for the storyteller to shout appropriate, sterilized truths in the soundproof safety of palatial or parliamentary courts, university ivory towers; or pit them against each other in the literary casinos of prize-halls where they anxiously await, albeit poised, the Russian-roulette of dispensations in the form of badges of honour and fame. They have packaged us in grants, residencies and scholarships. They have dangled an enticing array of flavourful prizes before our watering mouths to encourage the focus of our careers in the arts and define our literary life's value. From the smallest tidbit of brie represented by my local literature book prize (not to mention the full spread of actual wine and cheese at its award event), to the largest Caciocavallo cheese wheel of the Nobel Prize for literature, I can identify many tricks of the ruler's trade, seeking to bribe the artist and divert other possible focuses to their art besides entertainment, career advancement, accolades, ego-stroking. Alas, we mimic the corporate world of ladder-climbing for the sake of ladder-climbing, collecting prizes or bonuses as a measure of professional relevance and opus authority regardless of the incisiveness of the produced content. Most of us writers are also suffering from a crisis of values and of the spirit, a demoralizing decay which has contaminated most of contemporary life.

3. *revolution*

The social reality painted above presents me with a new truth. I am more effective in affecting the course of events that influence the lives of millions when I direct my narrative efforts at the nice, intelligent, learned, sometimes even sophisticated people who, despite not seeing themselves as oppressors, indeed are. The literate people who accumulate much power and privilege in the world hold the key to fundamental and lasting changes, were their awareness and consciousness to open and be directed by empathy rather than the goal of accumulating profit and amassing power.

I have known at aftershave-range men who have inordinate power over thousands or millions of people's lives as they collected fortunes beyond my comprehension. Inebriated by power and addicted to amassing wealth, they were well-spoken, practicing perfect manners, able to carry a pleasant conversation. They are also unwell and, as such, lost. Greed is a spiritual illness. Unrelenting power-hunger is an illness. Oppression and control are an illness. All these illnesses of the invisible heart are addictive, and very few addicts will raise their hand in a community and take responsibility for their addiction. They are caught in the thrall of their highs and many will not willingly desist from something they believe offers them a reason to exist, be it a syringe in their veins or more zeros in their bank accounts. They live in emotional and spiritual poverty and, unfortunately, they exert undue influence and direct many strings of the world. Don't misunderstand me. They can be very intelligent people and dynamic persuaders, which helps explain how they attained their level of wealth. Addicted to the game of arriving, they seem fooled by the deceptive life-map they have carried throughout their lives, and do not appear to mind the hamster wheel in which they live, the hamster wheel where there will never be a final arrival or everlasting apotheosis. Even power and success are ephemeral, as everything is, and therefore, one becomes caught in the unending vortex of cravings and addictions. Yet, they are the last ones wanting to hear they are sick. Denial, alongside a culture of validating and encouraging the illness of greed, will enable these people to continue these destructive patterns and behaviour.

4. *poetry*

After seven decades of existence, one such holder of inordinate power read for the first time a book of poetry. It happened to be a book of mine, for which he attended the launch out of politeness and in consideration of family ties. I know mine was the first, and most likely the last, book of poetry he read, considering he died a short few years later.

You might argue that having my words touch the ears of the powerful is a more miraculous task than to turn recycled motherboards into gold crucifixes. You might even add that had its rulers been capable of being touched by the words of others, the world would not find itself where the world is, on the verge of environmental and social collapse. People so excessively caught in the illusory game of amassing wealth for the sake of amassing wealth are the busiest of us all, finding little time to read anything but numbers, charts and financial reports, and no motivation to invest time and energy on a reading experience that will not add equity to their portfolio.

Some might have a point when defining these people as impervious and unreachable, although I believe in the decency of most human beings and count on the elites, as they age and mature, to realize there are limits to everything. Mortality approaches, and money, at this point in evolution, still cannot buy them out of everything, including cell degeneration. As they become vulnerable and taste mortality on their tongue, the door to empathize with all the vulnerable in the world may alas begin to finally open. This opening does occur, for most of us, wealthy or not. However, apart from this direct angle, I also see my words affecting the powerful from a lateral angle, even in the safety of their inner circles when they are not on guard. I mean, my stories can also reach their children, their spouses and their extended family networks, therefore influencing their circles of affection and those to whom they may be more responsive.

Perhaps they, and all of us, best remain open and responsive to feedback without the threat of confrontational attack and hateful chastising ringing in our heads. I respond best to change and re-evaluation when inspired by the stories that open my heart and remind me of my humanity and my capacity to connect and love, understand the world and others.

Perhaps I need to write compassionate stories about the hearts and the minds of the powerful so I understand them before the mirror that reflects how much of the world sees them, if they cared to look. We have had more than a hundred ice ages of storytelling and the world has not awakened. We continue to be savages in exquisite wigs or inside polished Rolls Royces; we have re-told every story about the suffering ones, the tortured and the hungry; and today I still count more hungry mouths than ever. Perhaps we need more stories about rapists and murderers, tyrants and torturers, misers and narcissists, stories which show the courage to delve into the depths of their pains and pleasures, denials and escapisms, their minds and beliefs, stories that follow their histories and their family histories, show us how we have or not have cared for their feelings or embraced their wounds, how we have punished and rewarded, as early as in the womb. Perhaps then we will begin to understand the universes they inhabit, to understand how we help create these people by the way we raise and teach them, feed their mind and body, so they act as if the rest of the world does not exist, so they act as if their actions do not destroy, so they act without care for the common good.

It is very possible we have treated these people without much sensitivity and they have never experienced unconditional care, not even in the womb, let alone in their cradle. Therefore they lack models of caring and of being responsive to others. Perhaps when I gather the courage to write about these dark universes that frighten me by venturing inside the horrors that shaped them, I will be arriving somewhere meaningful in my quest to understand these lives—all the while sidestepping the shallow and sensational gore-filled-narratives used to sell more publications by playing on people's fear.

The wealthy people I have known are not exceptionally crass, mean or monster-like, although they share a common trait. They know best and hold on to a paternalistic vision of the world and see themselves separate from the vast majority. They place themselves at the top of a stratified vision of hierarchies and abilities and perceive the human reality in black and white, in the same way they understand the ant colonies and bee hives of the world; it is incumbent upon them to rule and execute their personal blueprints of existence since they are a superior breed. This outlook separates them in a similar manner as it separates all humans from the rest of existence, with humans deeming themselves superior to other sentient beings and using others for our own means. From this place of separation all atrocities are born. The other—someone of a different colour, creed or sexual orientation; the other: lamb or tree—is always outside ourselves and does not belong to our universe of affections.

5. *strikes*

In this context, literature, theatre, visual art, cinema, music or any artistic endeavour which invests the creative spirit in bringing us stories of the past, present and possible futures becomes an essential tool to any transformative hope for our human societies and for human consciousness.

From a time even before I studied to become a lawmaker, having dreamt and believed in my ability to have an impact on my society by creating a more empathetic human planet through socio-political engagement within power structures, I have revisited with regularity the question of how am I to best contribute my skills to bettering the world. My early disillusionment with our political systems and uncompassionate civic institutions, which hold so tenaciously to achievements and power, membership and privilege, taught me that contemporary institutions existed to preserve patterns rather than facilitate processes for continuous evolution, transformation and fulfillment of the needs of our dynamic human consciousness and physical being.

Within institutions I found little room to breathe my distinctiveness and have unconventional ideas heard let alone embraced. Even the expected decorative ties at the neck, strangling my voice, were a reminder that I truly was on more than a mere symbolic leash. They called it a tie. Tied to what? To Whom? For what purpose? One dwells inside or passes through the norms of institutions to exit out the other side in the shape of another brick to add to its growing walls. In the process, we also help the institution to cement its authority by increasing its weight, height and rigidity. Institutions exist to ensure the continuity of its systems, not their disruption. Change is not their forte. These institutions exist to contain and anchor our achievements to serve a pre-determine objective we are not to question. Under their own weight and rigidity they become fossilized and non-responsive to our more limber and dynamic personal or civic needs. Institutions sit on solid foundations, yet they lack legs.

For the survival of my own spirit, instead, I decided to step into an alternative path. The allure of the arts beckoned with its open fields where the wind blew hair in wild shapes and colours. At least in the arts, I hoped to have a better chance of being myself. The authenticity of my free voice was the genuine gift that I could offer and which with luck the world might notice. If unsuccessful at inspiring the world, in the least, I would have a try at changing myself and saving me from institutional asphyxiation. By leaving law school, I had joined a vaster field of possibilities. No map, no assurances, no lines to tow and no regular paycheque.

In the past, many placed great hope in literature, song and theatre as vehicles for social and political change, and found promise in using the power of words, image and sound to stir the emotional bodies of the dissatisfied citizen into action. It was believed that if the story managed to touch the wound and transform the ache into hope, it would strike a nerve with the common folk and revolution would ensue.

6. *alliances*

We live in exciting times, times when the distribution and creation of stories has arrived in the hands of vaster and vaster numbers of people who had been silent, isolated and muffled within political geographies of oppression or restricted self-belief.

I do hold hope that those who have been silenced find access to the new tools of publishing so their ripened stories, however unpalatable to the status quo menu of authorized flavours, may now be heard. Since those people have nothing to lose, have no sales force to answer to, no literary careers to manage, juries to please, grant officers to be polite to, perhaps we will see the renascence of courageous narratives once again; and may they inspire the professional storytellers to step out on a limb and begin to dive into the depths of what people are longing for in their emptiness, discover their deepest aches and oppressions which must be expressed for the healing of our spirits and the well-being of our communities.

Meanwhile the floodgates of stories have already been opened, and now that I am on the verge of becoming overwhelmed by the barrage of stories to the point I want to cover my ears, what shall I do? What is the next evolutionary step of the story? Does it suffice to release the story and then release ourselves of the story, only to be filled again by the same story next week, the same pain, the same abuse, because the asphyxiation has not gone away?

Is the contemporary story another temporary pill we pop to ease the pain, though it will not free us as it should? Have we abused and diluted its strength as a powerful medicine, rendering it ineffective at these times we so desperately need it?

Telling my story, our story is no longer sufficient to transform reality, perhaps even no longer effective to vent or release the weight that drowns the storyteller, were I not to speak. It is not sufficient to just vomit a story.

In the same way that shouting my grievances on the streets releases the anger for a day, it is obsolete and ineffective to accomplish change. Yet, our imagination fails to find renewed ways to voice our collective concerns, to refuse to participate in that which keeps hurting us, to mobilize ourselves to rise from despair and ignite the fires of hope that will inspire and initiate effective change. We require new and creative solutions to both ancient and fresh problems. We require new, small, training steps to activate muscles long atrophied in apathy and despair.

General labour strikes, which had once been an important tool of protest and a catalyst for change, have now grown feeble as a pressure instrument for policy change. The strength remaining in marching on the streets lies in meeting each other, sharing our own stories and finding ourselves again, shoulder to shoulder, and escaping the isolation of the TV room. Insomuch as we find solidarity and renew our strength by finding our shared stories, demonstrations and gatherings will remain essential. They no longer break the steel arms of the powerful, although the volcanoes of anger do frighten them. They tolerate, manage and fence protesters in, allowing the steam of anger to whistle and roar on the streets while watched closely by their guard dogs of law and order. There is no law and order in the board rooms of corporations allowing forced factory labour, child labour, the poisoning of rivers and decimation of forests adding to their bottom lines. There is no law and order in the bankers' exclusive domains, no scrutiny of their rapacious practices no consequences to their manipulating schemes.

General strikes mostly hurt those who participate, those who have little to their name and, by protesting, lose further work days, wages or even their jobs. The powerful and the wealthy have built cushioning in their vast economic empires without borders, and will sit out any nuisance while dining *haute cuisine*. Labour strikes are the fly buzzing over their faces. It is the worker with little who cannot afford a week without pay. The deep pockets will close their factories, their services, shut food production down and move on to the next lackadaisical or corrupt country happy to accept the little crumbs of investment falling from the opulent laps, because logic of survival says, better a crumb than no crumb at all when children are starving. Those elites will be thanked and feel *charitable* and generous and almost human while releasing a burp of satisfaction.

As far as a first step in change, it is more effective to boycott the consumption of goods while simultaneously creating and strengthening our self-reliance. The essence of oppression begins, and is reinforced, by the economic system. If collectively, and step by step, we decide to shift our levels and patterns of consumption, and become more self-reliant for our basic needs, then we will affect the money-tap filling the tanks of wealth on this planet. At the same time we may choose or not to continue to work for the wealthy while buying time to create alternative forms of economic survival. Whatever our circumstance, we have varied ranges of manoeuvring which, with time, and each successive drop, may build a river. Growing food in grassy sidewalk plots or in balcony pots. Deciding not to buy what I don't need, which is most of what I buy anyway, from aftershave to tickets to sporting events or a new car. Instead, I will step outside the walls and play with my friends and our children at that sport I love. When I spend more time with others creating rather than consuming, promote alternative stories and visions of social equity, mutual support, I'll make the barons of wealth nervous. They will respond. We will need to prepare for their retaliation. Very few overindulged babies let their toys be taken away without a fair deal of kicking and screaming.

7. *very, very*

Who are these wealthy minorities who seem interested in defining the word and the world for me and you, and who are afraid of everyone else, chiefly the poor and of the great generic *masses* fuming with dissatisfaction on the streets? They have been successful at controlling the word because they own most of the TV, radio and book publishing avenues of the world and reach the majority of the population with their particular vision and stories of how the world should be.

Not afraid of writers at all, the wealthy easily lure us into tuxedos to dine and play bourgeois for a night in their company, while we politely write inane prize acceptance speeches and bow at the cheque. They know they have domesticated the storyteller. It is the worker marching on the street and the youth rebelling in front of Wall St. who they truly fear. History has shown that cyclical patterns of popular anger result in the loss of heads at the top; the chubby cheeks or austere noses have dangled from ropes or rolled away from the glinting guillotines. They have plenty of historical precedents to feel nervous.

At present the controlling minority is very, very afraid, and of course it will respond defensively to any suggestion of change. Expect that this *one percent* will step up resistance to change, through repressive legislative means and by the brute force of the armies at their service. They believe in a precise brand of story. They believe their story is the true and most important story. Their story is numbers and never has a face.

As any other defined minority, they are probably misunderstood and possibly also require special treatment. I am wise to understand the stories and their fears; I must reach them in order for this planet to survive before the much heralded Noah's deluge arrives and ends everything. When such day arrives it will be a flood of blood, not monsoon rains.

Let me practice transparency in my life before their strategies of concealment, let me practice generosity before their hoarding, let me even be generous with those who have everything but peace of mind, let me give things away, both the excess and the essential. Let us practice care for one another before their spears of fear. Let us share our stories, meaningfully. Many of us will fall, sacrificed to their fear disguised as anger, yet they cannot kill us all because they need a flock to run their factories, they need a flock to clean their houses and oil their machines, they need a flock to crave their merchandise. They cannot kill our stories.

8. *choices*

The wealthy require a flock of feebly educated citizens, unable to decipher the complex threads that weave modern society and unable to articulate strategies of citizenship that implement policies that truly address issues of socio-economic equality and justice. A citizen unable to dissect the complex relations of power, commerce, wealth and politics, is prey to the systems of persuasion, manipulation and disinformation that lubricate the system of inequalities and exploitations and therefore, naively, they will continue to vote and elect those who exploit them. This blindness arising from the lack of tools to clear the smoke screens bombarding them explains their counter intuitive actions against their self-interest. So they will also abstain from participating in alternatives that will address their suffering. These are the alienated citizens who have become essential for the dysfunctional working of our democracy.

That is why the powerful and wealthy are interested in education only as long as it prepares the worker bee to fulfil its task of economic production, and will fit seamlessly into the humming of economic activity designed to fatten the queen's profit. That is why the wealthy are not interested in investing in the humanities and the artistic education of the citizen. Citizens bearing a strong ethical and moral compass, an acute sense of justice and capable to articulate and deconstruct the fences erected around them, are not easy to influence, even less to manoeuvre, let alone manipulate. Power does not want the citizen to understand or question the language of power.

To equip myself with the skills of citizenship in order to participate in shaping our polis, I first need to invest in my education. The ability to access and decode information requires guidance, training and practice. Inane information aimed at distracting me, occupying my mind with irrelevant tabloid facts and sport statistics requires nothing of me. I become a passive bucket filled with data. Bombarding the citizen with inane information and facts is now an essential control mechanism in the (dis)information age. Instead, I need to be exposed to a wide diversity of views in order to learn the practice of independent and critical analysis, muscling up my ability to express complex thought patterns in order to arrive at my own evaluation of a situation for a more informed choice.

It is pointless to ask or expect me, as a citizen, to fully participate when I am ill-equipped. I don't want to dive into the depths of the ocean for any extended time while unable to read the currents or understand the bends, be unwise and unprepared for the specificity of such an environment, the dangers in the speed of ascent.

Those familiar with parenting strategies, striving to contain the effusiveness of children to fit the lesser worlds we have constructed, may recognize this common strategy of outlining the parameters of the available as an effective framework to limit human choice. Would you like this apple or this orange? Vote for party A or Party B? The attention is drawn away from the larger selection in the bowl of fruit, or worse, the vaster choices in the orchards of the world. This approach begins to condition the person to think, and then believe, choice is limited to the framework presented and no more. It's an effective way to limit choice.

With children, the strategy is applied to limit the understanding of agency in the process of generating choices. This controlled field of choice offers a passive response to an externally presented situation, versus an active, creative and internal process of evaluating one's genuine needs. This framework is introduced to condition and control, to ensure children comply to our world in order to manage and have them fit our existing lives. Often it operates for efficiency's sake, to ensure adult interests and priorities prevail. Our paternalistic and hierarchical social systems of household life mimic our democracies, of course. The needs of those with power take precedence over all others.

Our mass media also labours around the clock, broadcasting their condensed messages of choice with stern warnings, reminding us of our fortune in having a choice at all, all the while ensuring that we remain restricted to a limited menu, while feeling good and empowered, and well-distracted from more fundamental issues that may question power relations, wealth distribution and other essential rights of human dignity for all.

9. *crucification*
Who am I reaching with my words?

The writers who have mattered to me reveal themselves. They speak their truth. You know where they stand. They shine their light and reveal their shadow. The frailties and the strengths, fears and courage are worn on their sleeve, they are willing to focus on subjects most will not glance at from the safe distance of binoculars. These courageous writers turn every long-settled stone in my path, until then invisible, to show me the poison and the precious. Even those stones I kept tripping on and did nothing about because I did not know how to change my path and instead accommodated to live with the scrapes. My courageous writers are willing to question themselves, willing to explore who we truly are, and they dream beyond the ingrained beliefs of my understanding of the nature of things. I am what I believe I am. The relevant writers touch the wounds. Theirs and the world's. The relevant writers are willing to be *crucified* for what they believe, and likely will be. The relevant writers inspire and surprise me, they encourage me to seek my dreams, my essence, because they dared to seek theirs, and their narrative offered me another possible map, proving it could be reached. They have shown me a possible way; and mine is for me to discover. More than ever, I need to find out what I have become. What have we collectively become? There are more parrots in captivity than in the wild tangling with the wind. Is it time for a change?

10. *circus*

If I were to sit, day after day, in front of the distraction screen of the global mind, drinking its one-way delivery, I would not be creating solutions to our problems. Instead, I would be drowning out our problems from my consciousness, I would not be re-evaluating, re-imagining and re-organizing, I would not be helping to accomplish the change we long for. No, I would be arguing with you to exhaustion, with the fever of anger, whether the penalty call was truly a just penalty. Meanwhile, we could not argue justice face to face with those affecting us, telling them about the lack of fairness in our own lives, in our workplace, our communities. There is a reason the lords of the football foment ambiguity, in refereeing the rules of the game. They want to retain the element of human error, encourage the drama of ambiguity because it sells. It's an addiction and it permits manipulation of results when necessary to intervene; it is an essential tool to control the game from outside the game itself.

There is also story in every sport's game.

A repetitive, predictable story of anxiety and drama, justice and injustice, luck and bad luck, with a foreseeable outcome: a winner and a loser. After experiencing a few competitive sport games in the stands or as a player in the field, those sports soon stopped teaching me anything new. I would swing between disappointment and elation, much like a bipolar-afflicted patient. Competitive sport games are not stories that reflect the complexity of living where the winning and losing is never a clear-cut result of my cumulative actions. There are much better alternatives to teach me the skills of team work, cooperation and solidarity with everyone involved in problem solving, or to teach me strategies where everyone wins, and the collective needs begin to be addressed and fulfilled. Sailing treacherous waters in a catamaran or climbing a frozen waterfall will teach me skills that later may prove crucial to help rescue a sinking ship or retrieve wounded person. At best, in competitive team sports, if I am a winner, it will thrill the fans of my distinct tribe of allegiance, albeit temporarily so. I will desperately hope it lasts or I desperately hope its blessing touches me again and again in a miraculous benefaction of luck.

Why do we care so much about the utterly meaningless game of football? So much that we kill and hurt each other, families go without, and the frustrations of the game spill into the home, leaving bruises and broken bones on children, pets and women. If I disregard this human response to a mere game, I have failed. I have missed an opportunity to understand myself, my neighbours and something that affects my community life. I have failed to understand this human addiction to practices that generate enemies and adversaries in order to establish nucleuses of tribal cohesion; identity arising from warriorship as a primary or at times sole avenue for group identity affirmation. Politicians, rather than applying funds to eradicate child and old-age poverty or treat the mental illness roaming my city streets, will gladly divert limited public resources to finance luxurious stadiums or bail out sports teams in order to receive another mandate and satiate the appetites of the fans of this modern gladiator circus.

As in times of kings and gods and lords, I have placed my well-being in the hands of another. I have given my power away and I have also divested myself from the accountability of the outcome. I have been bribed by the candy of emotional addiction to sports. I can always blame the other: coach, player or referee, for the failings, while rejoicing over these victories as being my own.

Occasionally the stench of greed, injustice and inhumanity stirs even the most apathetic of us and in those rare seasons, we manage to let a grumble and ramble escape the silenced heart. We may complain and criticize with vehemence and passion from the safety of cushioned couches, assured that we face a TV without ears. These safe places, where the only movement on issues, the only movement on the moral being, is seen in the slight shift of the index finger pressing the button onward to the next channel of the equivalent stench. Nothing truly changes except the assurances and the narrative twists of stories without legs failing to inspire us to stand up and march for our dreams.

11. *pet-citizen*
The prevailing cultural diet, delivered through the immense reaches of electronic distribution, arrives in our living room with stories that support established patterns of belief. These narratives of centralized storytelling are tailored to polarize differences: friends versus enemies, good versus evil, poor and rich will always exist and continue to live worlds apart, and on and on goes the list. Endless divisions, in stories reinforcing our acceptance of fate, the immutability of the existing rules and religious precepts that define relationships and one's place in the social and political order. The heroes in these concocted stories feed us hope, without, in reality, achieving tangible change. We want to be convinced someone else, some other hero outside our living-room walls, is accomplishing the work of change for us, the work we need to be engaged in doing, rather than continue to experience the dread of sinking further and further into the sofa as the ring of fat around our waist grows larger. These storytellers and storymakers convince us justice will prevail, good overcomes evil, truth wins in the end, and Cinderella is an everyday reality. These narratives have become our daily inoculation to avoid full flare-ups of revolt. We are kept dreaming and soft on our couches. There is no action while we dream. From such dreams there is not a waking up.

My literary adherence to this official recipe of governing

the citizen by massaging the innocuous message into every pore of the brain would augment the chances of my creative works reaching mass commercialization, and therefore reaching that chimera of many storymaking artists: fame, name recognition, and of course, a respectful measure of wealth.

I hear from many fellow writers or teachers in the business of writing, this refrain: before setting word to paper one must identify what is selling, what the market wants. Writers are trained to serve and please the masses in order to eat and be loved. If the market wants potato chips, we'll serve them more chips until there will be little else available on the menu. If the market has been served excrement they will crave super-sized portions and improved flavours of the same. The work will be predictable, sanitized, sterilized, pasteurized and void of any living organisms, deemed safe for public consumption, and shrink-wrapped to land on our take-out lunch boxes. It is true, such food is mostly safe ... also dead.

To seek security and reliability is understandable. In order to put carrots on my family's table, a warm winter coat on my child, it is tempting to have reliable income. The child, too, will appreciate knowing what days they can count on having food on their plate. To ensure I deliver the predictable diet of anticipated results and no more, the *market* employs its hawkers: the agents, publicists and publishers holding the strings of cultural production. These gatekeepers have been deciding on behalf of readers what is worthwhile to experience. Commercial and financial values take precedence and rule over the artistic merit of any creative voice. If the book shows merit but is deemed not to appeal to sufficient numbers of people lining up at the cash register, the work is rejected as financially unfeasible. When ninety-nine percent of manuscripts land on slush piles and die there, book culture stagnates. Now that the cost of producing and distributing music, movies, visual art and books has diminished and brought it within the reach of millions more, the rules of the game have changed. The creators, through distribution channels such as Amazon.com, iTunes, and many others, have down-sized the number of people taking an inordinate chunk of their cake until, ideally, there should be a more equitable sharing among those bringing the book to life. Let's hope we can access the reader directly in the future and they will vote with their purchases. The gatekeepers are struggling to redefine and reinvent their role, to convince us again of their relevance to hold control of the puppet strings. Pinocchio has come to life, though; he now believes in himself and threatens to walk away free as any bird who leaves a wooden cage forever behind.

The gatekeepers of culture, by their meek vision, by their devotion to the paradigm, by design or as an economic side-effect of safe models of generating profit, have successfully held most alternative, challenging, incisive, fresh, innovative voices out of the eyes of the public.

There is an additional bright prospect in the opening of these publishing gates and the flood of voices pouring into the ears of the world. Among all of these voices there will be many raw and important stories and truths until now smothered under the authorities: be them political or the gatekeepers of the arts. In some societies they are one and the same. Perhaps these powerful stories will awake more professionals of the word to finally begin to take risks, to wade into those dangerous subjects that threatened to cut them off from the feeding bowl of the establishment. Yet, who will listen to this barrage of narratives, free filler for the profit-making providers of culture and social media? Are these stories being delivered with the skill they deserve to captivate the world and gain legs? The spectacle of everyone speaking at once in a traffic jam of shouting voices is only matched by the equal spectacle of no one left to listen with the true ears of listening.

I am not certain this will immediately or radically shift the menu of offerings in my cultural restaurant. One might simply become obsessed with the vast increase of the minute differences of the same dishes and spend the rest of one's life dining on the million varieties of burgers, and burgers alone, or watching the many football games being played in every field of every continent of every league and also never again change the channels of choice despite the six hundred and fifty-nine alternative offerings at my fingertips. In this way, the prison has merely been enlarged and the distance to the door grown that much longer. I may never again leave the living room and find the live culture on the streets among the breath of other citizens ready to digest a lively participatory exchange.

Presuming the framework of the internet and Amazon business models remain accessible and affordable to all, and that the cartel-like Amazon does not become the flytrap in a pending monopoly of book retail that will modify the rules of the game the moment it counts all in its clutch, then we have entered an era where the readers, listeners and viewers will hold the key to their own escape from these cages. Will I be obsessive and lullabied to self-indulgence in the quiet and warm pools of the familiar or will I be adventurous and willing to step out to new challenges and expanding horizons? The young, writers or not, and the actively dissatisfied, were traditionally the most likely to embrace opportunities to escape the cages, although these same groups are also caught in the nets of identity affirmation and recognition, struggling to be accepted and to fit into the adult world. Many are willing to conform and play the existing game just that much to the letter than their predecessors in order to impress and be welcomed by the status quo, with promises of immediate inclusion in the circles of privilege. Overwhelmed by the myriad of choices outside the cage, the warnings of countless real and imaginary, known and unknown dangers lurking, young and old will willingly lock themselves from the inside and settle in the cage.

I recognize that some of us will be satisfied living our existences in front of a sports game or Hollywood flick holding a beer in hand. Fulfillment arrives from many wells and the expression of meaning is subjective. Culture, science, religion and economics are not the only expressions of fulfillment. However, I hope there are more of us open and curious to find out what is beyond that door, that blank screen, that dark veil; willing to have our consciousness further awakened, our infinite possibilities revealed, strangled dreams resurrected by the imaginative key of storytelling, the creative impetus of invention; ready to be inspired out of inertia, drawn away from the mesmerizing and blinding glow of the TV room.

Conformity and lies are built of such dense matter that they sink any able body deep into the love seat at the end of the work day. The heaviness of conformity is such that it makes the black holes in the cosmos a matter of child's invention. It brings me back to what the market wants. I could write this book:

YOUR COUNTRY TROUBLE-FREE IN TROUBLESOME TIMES
Maintenance Manual for a Neutered Pet-Citizen

Or I could write another book.

Docile minds are not empty minds. Docile minds hum so very, very full of the nothing in meaninglessness, busy digesting ads, sport statistics, trivia contests with the laboured daze of ruminants ready for slaughter.

Dear citizen of our almost republic, you and I must be kept busy and our ears full. We must also be kept busy with the exhausting demands of a work and family life, and then for pretend relaxation and entertainment, while exhausted and vulnerable, be hypnotized by mindless storytelling of the glow-screen because we are more impressionable this way. The subconscious imprinting of swift branding images in advertisements, inane comedies, sports and soap operas likes me best in the marinade of beta waves. True leisure of doing nothing and generating alpha space around the mind must also be prevented. Unnecessary pauses in the hamster wheel of thoughts and mindless reactions signal potential breaches in the momentum of the programming. Pauses generate space in the mind. They stop the wheels and the flow. Out of nothingness, in the hollowness of this mind-womb, spacious creative energies emerge, and everything and anything can grow from that landscape without surveillance. Religion has warned us that creative thinking is the territory of the devil and therefore the geography of trouble and the damned. I am on my own in this barren (or is it barred?) landscape. Apparently, even God does not tread there with me, although we are told he is everywhere.

Are you keeping yourself busy and out of trouble? This order has been delivered to me in the guise of a question as long as I can remember. I better be busy or there will be a knock on the door asking me what I am up to. Stillness is no good. My desired silence, in particular, is no good. Only the officially approved brand of silence is approved. A defined silence. An understood and predictable silence.

11. *inertia*

Do my words; do my stories carry enough spark to lift people from the inertia of conformism and defeatism? Is it all up to me?

The moment has arrived when the dominance of imitative culture faces its death knell. Cultural diversity is no longer enslaved by exclusive economic forces of market patterns of production. An imitative culture is a dead culture. Now the gates have opened for a wider range of voices to step into the public arena and tumble the walls that have bounded culture in the traps of this economic game.

Imitative culture serves an important role in a political society interested in maintaining predictable, cohesive reigns on its citizens. It exists to anesthetize, to arrest people to their immutable realities, reinforce values, strengthen the cage around their horizons, reinforce the small windows, and convince them no other possible choice exists.

In this way it is not different from the cocaine in the vein that transports the consumer away from the mundane realities, neuters the gnawing anxieties and the hypnotizing doldrums of their ennui; imitative culture or cocaine mutes fears, gags the inferno of existence, and entrains hopelessness of true alternatives to life as is. The cocaine will deliver an user to the illusion of pleasure, to feel-good universes where reality seems to expand, power is tasted, and freedom and expansion of consciousness is glimpsed yet not sustained; hence the addict's craving to return to that delirious state with a borrowed and ephemeral key that is not her or his own.

12. *anger*

What has happened to the art of narrative or any other cultural expression which dares to startle and therefore awaken me by deviating from the expected diet? A narrative that surprises me, takes risks, touches wounds, says the unsayable and generates a twitch of discomfort—and therefore move me? Such writing often elicits resistance expressed as hate from those who have been rattled from the peace of their settled beliefs, those seeking reinforcements and confirmations and nothing else. They abhor the taste of uncertainty on their lips, the threat of the collapse of the world as they have known it, the shaking of the foundations, the loss of all that was.

Their anger is real, the fire in their eyes burns with the sizzling bite of frying oil. Their anger is real because their fear is real, their pain is real and their dread of collapse and annihilation is real. It takes courage to stand open to the shattering of my own identity, to become midwife to my own consciousness. This condition is often best accepted by force, when imposed by events deemed as acts of God, such as a devastating earthquake, an automobile accident, illness or any other near-death experience. It is seldom accepted by willingly stepping into the stream of change at another person's invitation. What, do you think I am insane to give up everything I built? Do you know the feeling of having your own skin peeled off while alive? Just look into the eyes of rabbits when that happens to them.

13. *emptiness*

Does the responsibility to shake those entertained to distraction or asleep on a sinking ship rest with me? Am I obliged to rescue those who chose to drink themselves into a stupor on a cruise ship? Am I, through my words, obliged to rescue others from their unhappy emptiness?

My responsibility begins with myself first. I am responsible to speak to those same places in me that are discontent and empty, those places silenced by my undiscerning acquiescence to authority without reason or heart. I am responsible to overcome the walls I have created or others have built around me, and then to share my insights, my failures and my successes on my narrative road to transformation and action. Alongside my culture, languages, and historic context that conspire to write my story, I am also the maker of my own story, and I also carry my oppressions and erect my own jails. All of us, no exceptions. In addition, we face several lifetimes of efforts to deconstruct the prisons of culturally generated stories. Although individuals among a collective flow and destiny, we each still have degrees of steering, and if enough of us jump the river bed, overflow the banks and the embankment, the course of the river will change. Together, we have carved a new river bed. If my words inspire, and the reader sees a reflection of familiar and unfamiliar places of silence in themselves, and wish to act, it is their prerogative to join the new collective flow.

I am also responsible to speak up and intervene when those who bear more weight at the helm of this spaceship earth, by virtue of their power, privilege and responsibility, fail to be accountable and to live up to their responsibilities. We share a collective destiny on this floating planet, and if our leaders fall asleep at the wheel, jeopardizing our wellbeing and crashing our planet, we must become even more involved than simply voting. In the same way that we deter irresponsible drivers on our highways, we should apply the same principles of competence to our economic, political and social engines driven by our elected or unelected leaders.

And most importantly: I am responsible to listen and listen and listen, before and after I speak my heart.

14. *men without*

I was raised in a culture of successive generations of men who have lost their ability to communicate meaningfully about our hearts and minds. As a consequence, we have lost our ability to be present with each other in order to build meaningful relationships. These relationships are essential to build trust and community strength in order to move together into spaces of change. The essential matters of the spirit, the flesh and the heart have been silenced, and my contemporary fellow men have resorted to the ultimate imbecility of our human condition: using up our precious collective time with each other arguing the fabricated dramas of sport rituals. Meanwhile our forests are burning down; a child dies of hunger every fifty-nine seconds; and by the time you finish reading this sentence several more women on the planet have been raped. Men spend their energy and emotions in the never-ending looped arguments of who is right or wrong, about the injustice of a penalty call which we cannot change anyway, while inebriated by the rivers of beer that flow out of our wallets.

We are men without. We are men without the tool of story. We are men without the courage of vulnerability. We are men in dire need of learning the weave of our stories, learning the power of sharing our experiences, injuries, fears, dreams. We are men overdue to express our frustrated, oppressed emotions, so we may complement the repertoire of our emotional tool-box with alternative options, besides punching or shooting anyone who challenges us. Not even when we break our bones, in the supposedly relaxed playfulness of sport, have we learned to feel the pain that fills our lives. We are deemed heroes the moment we bury our injuries behind clenched teeth and cover-up drugs, while playing on and on and on. Foolishly, we believe the bravado reflects a sign of heroism.

These are futile and dark times. We, the men, are angry. Anger is the only emotion we appear capable of expressing. We think we are angry at referees, budgets, politicians, laws, angry at everyone and everything. In truth we are angry at ourselves. Angry that we do not know how we erected the cages we find ourselves in, angry at the dead-end mess we have created, and too proud to fall apart and seek help to rid ourselves of this mess. Since we have been behaving like children, we now do not know how to be mature and acknowledge our failures and incapacities. Still too busy saving face, denying and pretending we know what we are doing, where we are going. We are utterly lost and afraid. We are afraid and we mistakenly believe it is a weakness to show we are afraid. We are also embarrassed. We are embarrassed because we do not hold the answers and the maps out of this mess. We expected more of ourselves; we believed ourselves bigger, smarter and more infallible than we actually are. We believed in the bravado of it all. We have never been accountable to clean up the messes, from baby diaper explosions to nuclear accidents, and it is time we grow up and start cleaning after ourselves and our responsibilities.

At which turn on the road have we forgotten that meaningful engagement with each other requires dialogue, and the courage that springs from vulnerability. Spectacle requires a silent spectator (or a brainless spectator chanting, hollering and yelling). Spectators are not agents of change, and they are not participants on the stage of events. They are only given the privilege of reacting and responding to the illusion that their feedback matters or influences the results. To follow or holler requires no brains. The time is here to reclaim our creativity again. Let us rise up from the couches of ennui, from the toothless meowing of complaining, say no to the eye-candy that hypnotizes us and join the conversations and hands on rebuilding that matter. We need you all, Creators with the backbone of spiritual and emotional meaning in our hearts, we need you to tell new stories, propose new visions to heal and serve our common good.

15. *the cage*

Let me be clear in my role as my own oppressor. How many times, of my own free will, have I stayed inside the cage because it was the road of less effort, easy and predictable, charming and full of immediate satisfaction? Too many times to count is the answer. I pretended I did not know the more lethal poison is the most insidious, the one which carries on undetected by the victim and over time seeps its way to the core as excessive salt or sugar will. Welcome to the kingdom of excess. Watch as the excessive consumption of liquor rots the body and asphyxiates the mind. Welcome to a world of obsessions that will trap us on the edge of no return. Watch the addictions rise, the despair spread in a tide of doom, that begins behind closed doors before it spills onto the streets.

The cage creates its own distortions. The oppressor is within and without. Many a time the door of the cage has been left open, only for the bird to remain inside, afraid of the free world they have never known, vast with possibilities and no map. I only need to observe the pet culture to encounter a representation of the larger scale of the dependency culture that humans have created. Habituation virtually guarantees very few will seek the freedom of independence beyond the guaranteed daily bowl of security. I too am a pet of the system that has toilet-trained me to expect what I expect after I pull my pants down. A paycheque.

I am the obedient writer who learned to obey word counts, guidelines, deadlines, industry standards of decorum, learned to rent tuxedos to attend the petting zoo of writers' prize ceremonies, learned to bow before the authorities and the royalties. I have learned to be polite and to refrain from offending editors, judges, publishers. I am the writer who wants to please the judges and serves them what they say they want. I am the writer who writes age appropriate words and nods and smiles before displays of nepotism. These social professional skills have served me well to navigate the world of art. Those skills are useful to fill the bowl in the cage. Now, the question arises. Have I equally cultivated the skills of disobedience, *enfant terrible*, thorn of discomfort so they are available in my writerly tool belt in order to remain awake, in order to escape the cage for fresh air?

16. *voice vs. image*

When I stop speaking up about what is important to me I have begun my journey to insanity. I have also begun to die.

In the end, I will write from my conscience and my desire to contribute to any meaningful understanding of our existence. I will attempt to balance earning a living in the physical world of carrots and seasonal hats for the brain, while leaving this earth a greener and a more conscious, just, equitable, social milieu for the next generations. The measure of wealth and sales shall never become my impetus to set word to story. Book prizes, book sales do not reflect the impact of my words in our society. What matters to me are the lives that will be touched and transformed by my words, the influence and inspiration, resistance and counter-arguments they have generated, the conversations and other words they have spun that in turn might become even more transformative to our existence and the larger non-human reality. Most of this outcome will largely be immeasurable, untraceable, never known, least of all by me. I do not need to know, because the gifts I need to share will be shared. My words will have grown beyond their creator, detached themselves and formed their own separate lives.

No individual story is immortal, none. Storymaking as a process of human expression, however, will remain immortal. In the same way, you and I are not immortal, yet life itself as a generative and regenerative impetus is a never-ending process.

Author photos in books, a grueling schedule of public appearances across the country, and the cult of personality attached to cultural creation have brought writers to the status of commodities to be sold alongside the objects they have created. Electronic books will soon carry the face of the author in video interviews, footage of their private lives. Intimate details of their family will add to the cult of personality and fuel the era of ego-inflation. The ego seeks admirers; the spirit seeks contact, interlocutors and exchanges. In this gap, most of us writers will trip and fall, buried by time until innocuous and irrelevant.

This emphasis on ego has distracted the storymakers from the true labour, which is the most important because it is unencumbered by the distractions of vanity.

17. *beautician*

As an inventor of stories, a scribe of events and beautician of words, my vocation is replete with responsibilities. The quest of insight matters to me. I invent stories to unveil the obscured surfaces of a canvas concealed by the massive pollution of other narratives dumped into the collective cultural space by charlatans interested in fogging up the understanding of the world.

In a time when the word has been diluted, dulled, neutralized, the word diverted to focus its energies on muddling events or to sell me the chewing gum and cigarettes I do not need; the task of reviving language is a transformative act. I must energize the word by applying words with authenticity in order to illuminate, respecting the word's intention as vehicle to deepen communication and understanding among humans.

Perhaps I would be more effective were I to attempt to understand the elites or the aptly named 1% who control and devour the world. Perhaps the writing which carries more socially transformative impact is the one read by those who fear the writer, and not by the people living in misfortune. The latter show little disposition or patience to digest the nuances and complexities of intellectual literature. Those who feel threatened by the truth, those who fear a writer are our most attentive of readers, the censors—by our divergence from the message they want everyone to accept. In my wildest dream I am read by those afraid of change, because things as they are translate to privilege, power and control over their reality. They, as most of us, do not wish a very, very succulent privilege stopped. Will I, the writer, stand in the way of compliance?

Will I be able to approach the elites with bare hands and tell a story of the world they may not wish to hear and without threatening their pristine sense of selves, their comfort zone? Is that possible or desirable at all?—The stench of the open sewers, the black tar sticking to dolphins and urchins, the screams of the politically tortured impacting their pristine view of the aquamarine swimming pools in their tropical vacation homes, I suspect, are not the literature of choice held by sun-screened hands and manicured nails. Such distasteful views of the world are abhorred amid exclusive ClubMed bubbles of existence?

Or will I be able to weave a wondrous, magical story of *fairly* tales and happy endings that somehow will awaken the elite's hidden humanity from within, and in time, in metaphorical ways, lead them with new hearts to those very same sewers. Is it possible for me to engage their attention long enough so they want to hear the yarn of the complete story unravel until they discover the concealed bullet and the red-stained thread in the middle of their daily actions? Would they want to hear that and would they do anything about it?

Will I be skilful with my words, capable of showing

through narrative what I perceive so those wealthy others will glimpse the world through my eyes? For an instant their reader's eye is invited to listen inside another's heart, long enough to be touched by the lives of those affected by their far reaching wealth and actions? Will I succeed in conveying the understanding that caring for others is also caring for oneself, since we are interdependent? That the preventable suffering or grief that exists far away from our consciousness, yet just on the other side of our walled mansion, does touch all and makes our planet a lesser place; regardless of the height and thickness of the walls, regardless of the bubbles invented to shield us from the unpleasant?

I, like most, also fear the loss of expected comforts and privileges, and what I do not know. Am I not sufficiently skillful with my words to let the wealthy know through my *brilliant* literature that there is life after their very hands have cleaned their toilet bowl for the first time? That they will enjoy eating again the week after they have changed their children's first diarrhea diaper? That scrambled eggs in reality are not that difficult to mess up? The point is to mess up. They could start there: they already have experience with messing up. I know the fear of failure is elevated for those in high pedestals, and anxiety already weighs on their nights. Many lean on the bottle and the pills for a variety of reasons; and that makes my task that much more complicated. They are not fully present.

Will my words transform their mindset of scarcity to one of sharing, from exclusivity to inclusivity, of unhealthy individuality and narcissism to communal wealth and health? I can only be a healthy individual in a healthy community, as I can only be a healthy cell in a healthy body. In the same way we share air and water, we also share psychic spaces of ease or disease.

I am aware of the enormity of what I am requesting of myself and requesting of every other human being. I am asking us to strive for another state of heart and state of being, asking us to awake to a sensibility that invites every one of us to hold the well being of everyone and everything on the palm of our hand as we conduct the actions of everyday life. It is only when we stop gazing at out belly buttons and perceive our self-interest as separate from the self-interest of the cosmos that we may find a path out of the labyrinth of cyclical torments that have haunted the human condition from time immemorial.

In the writing of this text I have already convinced myself of the urgency of fearless, compassionate narratives. Those words I am yet to learn in order to appeal to those who most need to hear them. Once I do become fluent in words of wisdom I will be telling these earth-shattering stories pronto, right? After all, if not me, who? If not now, when?

Until today, when I sat at the breakfast table, listening to the news of gold prices going up and interest rates going down. I felt elated by the news of mortgage relief as the hot chocolate touched my lips and the unreported stories of boy soldiers in gold mining Africa echoed in my unconscious. Then I realized I am not inventing these stories for my readers. I am telling stories for me, for those around me, from family to friends. I am teaching myself to unravel and follow the long thread of the impact of my actions—the skill of empathy—teaching myself to understand the kaleidoscope of human beings in order to understand the world and untangle the yarn of everyone's story. Yearning to wake myself up from the membership of those fearing war, fearing poverty, fearing violence; wake myself up from all those anxieties of change, concerns over whether I can hold on to the roof over my head, my holidays and my air travel, the restaurants and concerts and theatre I choose to attend. This is also a life of privilege which I had believed belonged only to others. I can look up the ladder and I can look down the ladder, and still I do not know where I stand. I too am seen as an oppressor by many. Because of the country I live in, because of my profession of letters; for having a roof to my name, and dessert after my meal; by the palette of choices available to me. I have a long road to write upon before I can change myself, let alone imagine I can change you, my reader.

Victoria / 2011

These essays, thoughts, inner conversations, arguments and rambles, have been written over the course of the past twenty-odd years and depict the evolution of my reflections on subjects of individual and cultural identity, the role of literature and authors in our societies as well as the challenges faced by those of us in the profession of letters.

Over the years I have benefited from the friendship and collaboration of many friends and colleagues who kindly offered feedback on earlier drafts. My thank you to Heather, Nowick and Galen. A nod of admiration to Greg for being a good sport despite the verbal rebuke.

In earlier incarnations and under different titles two of these essays were first published in the Banff Centre Press anthology entitled: Beyond Words. A third essay was also published, in Portuguese, by Revista Esquina do Mundo.

ABOUT THE AUTHOR

paulo da costa was born in Angola and raised in Portugal. He is a bilingual writer, editor and translator living on the West Coast of Canada. paulo's first book of fiction, *The Scent of a Lie*, received the 2003 Commonwealth First Book Prize for the Canada-Caribbean Region, the W. O. Mitchell City of Calgary Book Prize and the Canongate Prize in Scotland for the title story. In Portuguese he has published a collection of poetry, *notas-de-rodapé* (2005). His poetry and fiction have been published in literary magazines around the world and have been translated to Italian, Chinese, Spanish, Serbian, Slovenian and Portuguese. His latest book of fiction is *The Green and Purple Skin of the World*, Broadview Press / Freehand Books (2013). As a translator paulo has brought to the English-speaking readers a range of Portuguese poets including Nuno Júdice, Al Berto and Daniel Faria. To the Portuguese-speaking readers, and among others, he has translated the Canadian poets, Margaret Atwood, Michael Ondaatje, Gary Geddes, Patrick Lane and Marilyn Bowering. *The Cartography of Being*, Selected Poems of Nuno Júdice 1976-2005 (2012) is his latest book of translations.

www.paulodacosta.com

BIBLIOGRAPHY:

Books
Beyond Bullfights and Ice Hockey: The Architecture of a Multicultural Identity - *essays*
The Green and Purple Skin of the World - *fiction*
The Scent of a Lie - *fiction*
The Cartography of Being, *poetry* Nuno Júdice translated by paulo da costa
Midwife of Torment and Other Stories - *fiction* (forthcoming)
bifocal *poetry* (forthcoming)
The Waters of Remembrance *children* (forthcoming)

Audio Books
Midwife of Torment and Other Stories *fiction*
Twenty Poems *poetry*
The Book of Catalogues *fiction*

Livros
O Perfume da Mentira *ficção*
notas de rodapé *poesia*
eco (lógico) (no prelo) *poesia*

Livro Áudio
notas de rodapé *poesia*
XX Poemas *poesia*
ser português *poesia*

www.ingramcontent.com/pod-product-compliance
Lightning Source LLC
Chambersburg PA
CBHW031158270326
41931CB00006B/319